GW00986557

A Song From L'Abri

Other books by Betty Carlson
from GOOD NEWS PUBLISHERS:

Absolutely and the Golden Eggs

Of Mice and People

Right Side Up

A Surprise for Bellevue
  with Jane Stuart Smith

A Song From L'Abri

by Betty Carlson

GOOD NEWS PUBLISHERS
Westchester, Illinois 60153

Library of Congress Catalog Card Number 75-16653
ISBN 0-89107-000-1

First published in Great Britain by Hodder and
Stoughton, under the title *A Singing Heart*,
copyright © 1972 by Betty Carlson.

American edition, revised, copyright © 1975 Good
News Publishers, Westchester, Illinois 60153. All
rights reserved. Printed in the United States of
America.

Front cover photo: Edwin Adams. Upper back photo:
Marilyn Herring. Lower back cover photo: Edwin
Adams. Design: LTD.

To Liggie, a wise-hearted gentle lady from Virginia, radiant with faith, and to Jane Douglas, also a Virginian, unique, imaginative and an enthusiastic child of God, who every time we met in the past few years asked if *the book* was finished when it had not even been begun. I give thanks to God for these good friends and many others.

"I will sing unto the Lord as long as I live:
I will sing praise to my God while I have my being."
PSALM 104:33

Contents

Prologue

Finiteness is limiting. One can be in only one space at one time ... one can only do one thing at one time ... and there is a reality about being able to live only one life! Curiosity makes us want to experience someone else's life, at times, because of the unity and diversity involved. There is a unity in being a human being among other human beings, and a diversity in realizing that no two people are alike, nor are two lives identical. There is nothing quite like reading a vivid story of the actual history of someone else's life to give one an opportunity to identify, at least in a partial way, with a totally different set of circumstances, as well as to recognize one's own experiences are there too.

In case you have never been an opera singer, this book will let you live through portions of the life of an opera singer with its excitement, struggles, fulfilments and emptiness. You will experience the strenuousness of study and practicing, as well as thrill to the applause and glamor of first nights. You can travel with Jane Stuart Smith in Egypt and Greece, as well as live in Italy. You can sing in America, Palermo and Nice, as you live in these pages for a few hours. More than this, you can recognize something of your own search for an absolute ... for truth ... for a real way of living ... even while denying the existence of an absolute by conforming to twentieth-century relativism. Perhaps you can also identify with the finding of truth, or perhaps your own story has not included such certainty.

This book reveals far more than one period of one person's life ... as it really demonstrates the diversity of the specific dealing of the living God, who is personal as well as infinite, with human beings who have need of being treated as personalities and not machines. Who but a PERSON would care to arrange details to bring a seeking person to a tiny chalet in a mountain village to hear and see the answers to honest, agonizing questions that involve all of life?

Betty Carlson is the one to tell this story, not only because she knows Jane and has shared Chalet Chesalet with her for many years, but because she herself knows the reality of the infinite, personal God who cares to weave together events and lives like threads in a tapestry in answer to the individual requests of His children, as well as according to His plan. Words can capture only a portion of any one moment, even as photographs can. A book can only give glimpses into periods of a life ... and a book about a living person has no real ending, only a kind of beginning to a continuing story. In a way it is a tremendous fact that life-to-death too is only an introduction to the story that cannot be told about anyone, that is, the eternal period ahead.

Jane is still living in Chalet Chesalet and her voice rehearsing scales in the kitchen often mixes with the sound of a typewriter from the study above. The practicing indicates that music is still a real part of her life, but in a different setting, for different reasons, and combined with a different blend of people. Far from being an "ivory tower," this alpine village is the location of L'Abri Fellowship, which often seems to be the crossroads of the world to personalities from a tremendously diverse mixture of races, nationalities, ages, types, philosophic, cultural and religious backgrounds, who meet together in discussion and study, in times of working in gardens and kitchens, in sipping tea or eating meals, in singing, laughing and praying in the various chalets—each a shared home.

The musician and author share their home in the L'Abri community, and Jane's voice is not only heard in concerts and church services, but in giving art and music lectures, and in asking a student to clean out the chicken house or help her weed the garden. The diversity of a writer and a former opera singer sharing their creative talents in making a home, makes the chalet interesting indeed, even as the reality of oneness is demonstrated in a unity of purpose in the objectives of L'Abri. The variety of the homes in this community helps to demonstrate the excitement of diversity. This is not the story of a cog in a machine ground out of a bigger machine, but of a human being who has significance in history, written by another human being who is also significant in the real universe.

It is refreshing in the twentieth century to read of such a life in *A Song From L'Abri* rather than be depressed by another tiresome book about a painted-on smile of a singing clown who is miserable, written by an equally miserable, disillusioned person debunking history. Betty not only knows the life about which she is writing, but she too knows the Person from whom changed lives come.

Shortly after the title was chosen, Jane was taken to the hospital in the valley with a smashed ankle, all plans for the summer disrupted, and facing long months of pain and limping, but the "song" was still there, not coming from her lips, but from the depths of her heart. This astonished and made glad the Swiss women who shared her ward, as well as the nurses and doctors and many friends who visited her. Betty, herself, I must add, learned something too of the reality of adjusting to and accepting changed plans, and so a singing heart belongs to the author as well as to her subject. Just as Jane's Italian Maestro (about whom you will soon be reading) prepared her for her opera debut, so is the Eternal God training us through our good and bad experiences for our future lives with Him.

Edith Schaeffer

A Song From L'Abri

1
A Night in Venice

"**W**here have you been and what have you been doing, Maestro?" snapped the tense, young singer as she stood in the center of the dressing room while her mother was sewing pieces of jewelry on her green satin gown and a maid was kneeling at her feet arranging the long, lacy mantle of the costume.

"Where have I been? Per carita! What have I been doing?" exploded the Italian as he walked nervously around the singer inspecting every detail of the costume, and particularly the headpiece to make certain it was securely fastened on. He raised his arms and kept waving them as he said, "I've been haggling over the price for the 'claque,' and talking to the conductor and explaining the stage movements to the prompter, calming down the chorus, arranging the party for you at La Taverna and ... what have I been doing? Mah!"

"What's a 'claque?' " interrupted Mrs. Smith. Although she had been following her daughter's career with great interest, this was her first visit to Italy. Both she and Maestro, while they were talking, had their eyes fixed on the headpiece as the singer threw back her head to swallow a raw egg.

"Bravo!" said Maestro. "Now I'm convinced your

17

headpiece won't fall off. Say, did you have your vitamin shot at the hotel and your...."

"Tell mother about the 'claque,' Maestro. She's never been to an opera in Italy, you know."

"Oh yes, the 'claque,' " Maestro said, rarely taking his eyes off the costume to be sure everything was exact. "There are thousands of people out in the audience waiting to hear your daughter, Mrs. Smith, and they have to know when to clap." He paused a moment as he inspected the soprano's long, plastic fingernails. Then he looked increduously at Mrs. Smith and said, "You mean, really, that you've never heard of the 'claque'? You dear Americans, you are naive, and you are wonderfully innocent! In Italy we have to pay people to applaud at the right places and to keep clapping to stir up enthusiasm. If you don't pay," he shrugged his shoulders, "they will whistle, boo, talk loudly and ruin the performance. It's a horrid custom, but you can't beat it. Even Caruso spent a fortune on the 'claque.' "

At that moment a stagehand knocked on the door to announce that it was nearing curtain time. Maestro stepped directly in front of his student to give her one last critical look. Then he took her by the hand, being careful of the long fingernails and led her to the door.

"Are you ready, cara?" he said gently. "The gondola is waiting."

The year was 1951 and the place, Venice.

All about the famous city of canals were large, colorful posters announcing the opera *Turandot* with the leading role to be sung by the young American soprano, Jane Stuart Smith. There were even notices posted on several of the old but still beautiful palaces which recalled the days when Venice was the Queen City of the Adriatic. For her European debut Jane was singing one of the most difficult of all soprano roles. There was excitement among the opera-lovers waiting

18

in the outdoor theater near St. Mark's Square to see and hear if the much publicized American had the voice, strength and dramatic ability to sing Turandot.

Her teacher knew better than she the risk involved in having a young singer attempt a precarious role before a Venetian audience. He knew that if she did not succeed, they would not only boo her off the stage, but finish her in Italy for years to come. His reputation was at stake too, but he also knew that if his singer lived up to his expectation, she would capture Italy in one performance. Italians love to exaggerate, to do the BIG thing. Maestro was very Italian.

To be a successful opera singer in Italy is a big thing. Maestro was aiming high. It was a bold stroke, but both the teacher and the pupil loved to dare, and after all, he was not shooting in the dark. He had worked with Jane (she thought unmercifully at times) but he insisted that there was no other way to success than discipline, work, repetition and single-mindedness. She had come to him with a voice already superbly trained, and he had gone on from there giving the best he knew.

As he helped Jane into the gondola by the red and white striped mooring pole near the theater, he adjusted one of her gold lamé gloves. "Gently," he said, "step down gently, cara."

It was a delicate maneuver settling her into the gondola, but this was part of the pageantry of Venice. It would have been much simpler for the star to dress near the outdoor theater, but that would never do in the city renowned for its color and romance. In Venice the leading lady must arrive at the theater square in a gondola. The lovely satin and brocade costume with the trailing, hand-painted mantle sparkling with jewels had to be carefully draped over the extra seats. Jane was of no help because of her oriental fingernails. Maestro gave one final glance at the headpiece and stepped lightly aside so pictures could be taken. As the gondolier pushed off from the dock, Maestro smiled at his pupil and called after her, "Enjoy the ride! I'll meet you at the square in a few minutes."

As the gondola moved swiftly down the dark canal towards the outdoor theater, she began to think. Why in the world am I here? She disliked these moments alone when her mind would run restlessly over a familiar set of questions, and then she started agonizing over what was immediately ahead of her. Because it had rained during the past week, she had not had the benefit of rehearsing outdoors. All the rehearsals had been in the Opera House. Her thoughts were confused and gloomy. She wished Maestro was with her, but there wasn't room because of her costume. He tried to keep her cheerful before a performance, or at least they could have an argument. That was almost as good! As she looked into the water reflecting the lamps from some of the mysterious palaces which line the Grand Canal and which have been there for hundreds of years, suddenly she thought of Wagner.

He had come to Venice because of an unfortunate love affair, and it was in one of these palaces he had written the duet for *Tristan and Isolde*. Years later, in another palace, the tormented composer had died.

Even before she began studying opera, Jame knew that this was her ambition, to sing the great music of Wagner. His music was her passion. Her singing in Italy was only a springboard to the Wagnerian dramas which were written for her voice. She had tried to express this longing to Maestro, but he had no love for the German, so they rarely discussed it. But underneath it made Jane as ambitious as Maestro to make the Venetian performance a triumph.

As the gondolier steered the craft into a narrow canal, the full moon came into view. The gondola slipped under a graceful bridge. The beauty, the

20

unbelievably romantic setting, the enchantment of Venice caused the singer's gloom to disappear. She laughed out loud. This made the gondolier laugh too. He began to sing a Venetian folk song, but the magic moment was brief. Ahead she saw a brightly lighted landing place. Solemnly the gondolier announced, "Signorina, we have arrived."

As Maestro helped Jane out of the gondola, he was about to give a last word of advice, but he didn't say a thing. The face he was looking into was not his pupil, it was Turandot, the beautiful, cruel Princess of China.

The full moon poured a golden light over the stage as Princess Turandot made her spectacular entrance and the huge crowd strained forward to hear the tremendously difficult "In This Palace." As the crescendos began to build in the orchestra, Jane's voice soared higher and higher and the climactic high "C" was followed with a spontaneous burst of applause. The American singer had captivated her audience.

When the performance was over, many in the audience came forward to personally congratulate the young singer, and most significantly of all, there was an impresario from Palermo with a contract in his hand for her to sign. He was extravagant in praise and promised Jane and Maestro that a whole new production with original sets and costumes would be waiting for her to sing Turandot in his beautiful, large theater, and off they all went to the elaborate supper party at La Taverna to celebrate the triumphant debut in the golden city of canals.

2
Lots to Do

Jane had every right to be tired as the train pulled into the noisy Milan station. It had been a strenuous week. Besides the long frustrating rehearsals, she had walked all over Venice. She loved visiting art museums. She was charmed with the narrow "streets" and the many bridges, the glass factories, the shops full of ancient treasures, the festivity of St. Mark's Place, the grandeur of the Doge's Palace. Then there had been the big party at La Taverna which had lasted until the early hours of the morning. But in spite of all Jane was the first one off the train and had a porter at her side by the time the rest of the weary party came out of the coach.

Maestro suggested, "Let's stop and have an espresso."

Again it was the young opera singer who led the way across the high-arched station to a coffee bar. Many eyes turned to look at the tall, handsome American in the attractive green linen dress. Her carriage was erect, her head high and she walked with a determined, yet graceful stride as if she had something important to do. But Jane was not a conceited person. This was not her character.

While Maestro and the others stood at the bar slowly stirring quantities of sugar into the strong, black coffee,

Jane threw back her head and in one gulp downed the espresso. Maestro shook his head, "You shouldn't do that, cara. Think of your vocal chords! With a raw egg, yes, but coffee, never!"

She laughed heartily and said, "Come on, let's go. I have lots to do today."

Maestro continued to sip his coffee.

"Oh," he said, "so you have lots to do today, young lady. Most interesting, but I have other plans for you! You are going straight to the hotel to rest."

He went on, "I've given your mother strict orders. No shopping, no museums, no phone calls, no visitors, no spaghetti, no pastries—only a little soup and tea tonight!"

He looked at Jane intently. "We begin work tomorrow for Palermo, and we're going to work harder than we've ever worked before. So you were a big star last night, fine, but now you have to live up to something. That was only the beginning. From this time on opera is your god and we're going to eat, sleep, dream and live it!"

Jane had been looking into her empty coffee cup all the time Maestro was talking, and her face became more and more clouded. For a brief moment it looked as if she were going to defy her teacher, but almost immediately she gave in. It was not easy for Jane to take orders; in fact, she was usually giving them, even to Maestro on occasions. But when it came to the future of her opera career, she was childlike and trusting.

While they waited for a taxi, Mrs. Smith and Maestro were discussing the time to practice tomorrow. When the arrangements were finished, Jane said, "Maestro, please, I just want to walk through the park," hurriedly, she added, "It relaxes me, and I promise I'll come right back. Honest!"

"You are a child," he said kindly. "I'll give you thirty minutes."

They let Jane out at the zoo entrance which was a short walk from the Manin Hotel where Jane and her mother were staying. As the driver pulled away from the curb, and the taxi blended into the traffic, Jane waved at Maestro, who was leaning out of the window pointing to his watch. Jane smiled, then turned and walked energetically towards the elephants' cage. She sighed. It was marvelous to be on her own, even if it was only for half an hour.

As much as Jane loved singing and had already shown her willingness to work to develop her talent, her voice also was a burden. It imposed such limitations. She thought, "Imagine, at my age, being told everything I can and cannot do, mostly, cannot do." She stopped at a small kiosk and bought a triple ice cream cone and ate it with delight chanting to herself, "You mustn't eat ice cream, Bella Salamona,* nor speak on windy streets, in drafty halls, in chilly rooms...." By the time she approached the elephant house, she was in a carefree mood.

Jane loved animals. Although she had lived mostly in cities, she had spent her childhood summers on a farm in the Blue Ridge mountains of southwestern Virginia. Here she learned to dig potatoes, hunt eggs, ride horses and climb mountains. The evenings were spent in front of a large fireplace where stories were told and books read, and dreams dreamed. There was a love for fine literature in this country home, and Jane developed a lifelong habit of reading widely.

She smiled a little when she remembered the day she wrote to Aunt Betsy and asked if she could buy Dixie. She and the lively young horse had been inseparable all summer, and when the time of parting had come, it had been nearly as dramatic as a scene from a Wagner

*Bella Salamona (Maestro's favorite name for Jane) is an Italian expression of tenderness and endearment. The literal translation is beautiful salami which reveals a great deal about Italian values.

opera. When she was back home in Roanoke, she began saving money; and one day she wrote and asked Aunt Betsy if she could buy Dixie.

She explained that she had almost enough money—three or four dollars—and she was positive her parents would approve, although she hadn't exactly talked it over with them yet. There was plenty of room for a horse at their home. He could stay on the front porch tied to one of the columns. Well, it was true, she admitted, that the chickens she had brought home from market a few weeks before had not lasted long, but that was because the neighbors objected to the noise.... It was one of the singer's big disappointments in life when she was not allowed to buy Dixie....

Jane hurried on towards the cage for elephants. She did not want to miss the piano-playing act. It always amused her, but this time when the elephant lumbered out and at the crack of the trainer's whip began cranking the handle on the mechanical piano, suddenly she did not feel like smiling. She thought, "The world thinks it's so exciting to be in the theater, and in a sense I don't have much more freedom than this poor animal turning the handle."

Jane walked slowly away from the zoo towards the lake. She was deep in thought. It did feel good to be in the open air, and she breathed deeply as she walked on the grass among the giant trees.

Jane had already spent a number of years in New York City where she had attended Juilliard School of Music and also studied with several private teachers. Even though there was a part of her exuberant nature which did respond to the excitement of a large, noisy city, she was already beginning to be suffocated by the surface glamor and intoxication of the theater and its artificiality. But she recalled there were wonderful moments too, like her American debut in grand opera in Detroit. Her performance was hailed as the Festival's best. Being the daughter of the president of a railroad company, it is true she had the support of a private carload of well-wishers, which included all the members of her family, many friends and other relatives. But as a music critic of the Detroit *Free Press* said, "The paternal gesture is easily understood, though it was not a necessity for the success of its recipient. For Miss Jane Stuart Smith doesn't need any aid in the furtherance of her career as a dramatic soprano. Miss Smith is a woman of commanding beauty, both of person and voice...."

It was also in Detroit that a reporter asked Jane if she intended to go on using her own name professionally. Before the singer could answer, her mother retorted, "Why not? That's her name, isn't it?"

Jane did run into difficulty with her name in Ancona. Maestro protested when they noticed that her last name had been left off all the publicity, but the impresario was adamant. He said that Smith was a German name, and no German was going to sing in *his* theater. He liked the name Stuart though, because that was a royal Scottish family name, and the impresario liked the Scots.

Later Jane discovered that the Germans had bombed some theaters during the war, and for that the Italians of Ancona could not forgive them. Public buildings, museums, factories, yes, but to bomb a theater, unforgivable. As Jane told a reporter in Detroit, "Music is the soul of Italy. Everybody goes to opera. Theaters are as numerous and popular as American baseball diamonds."

The main thing for Jane, whether she sang as Jane Stuart Smith or Gianna Stuart, was how she was accepted, and the good part of her career and the portion she was beginning to enjoy were the rave reviews that were appearing in the Italian press. She

26

came out of her reverie and rapidly began walking towards the hotel. As Maestro said, "There's much hard work ahead." All thoughts of the brief glory she had enjoyed were pushed out of her mind as she wondered how to explain her tardiness to her mother.

3
Act Like a Prima Donna

The next morning when Jane entered Maestro's studio, he remarked how well and rested she looked.

"I ought to," she said. "I feel like a caged panther, and I'm starving!"

"Benissimo!" Maestro said with enthusiasm. "That's when a prima donna works the hardest. Come along, cara. You'll be glad you're rested!"

He added, "After our lesson, Signora Rolandi has a treat for you. She's in the kitchen now fixing your favorite dish...." He put his finger to his lips, "but I'm not supposed to tell."

The lesson began calmly. Maestro told Jane to stand in the corner and sing a simple melody, so she could hear her own voice. "Listen, listen, listen." Then they went through several scales with Maestro pounding a note or two on the piano to establish the pitch.

There was a cigarette smoldering in the ashtray hooked on to his music stand, and as he hit another note, only it was the wrong note, ashes spilled over the keys from the cigarette in his mouth. He said, "I want to hear that B flat!"

"I am singing B flat, Maestro. I don't know what you're striking!"

"Sing it out!" he shouted.

Maestro, beloved teacher that he was, had many inconsistencies. One of the rules he preached the loudest was the "no smoking" one, and the first thing he would do in a lesson was light a cigarette, and as the lesson picked up in tempo, the smoking increased.

He made a few more wild slams at the keys, and finally found the note he was after. As he walked back to his stand, he muttered, "I thought you had sharped, but I guess you hadn't."

He lighted a cigarette, "Your top notes are still not round. Color them, open them up, and stop leaning on that chair. You're not going to have anything to hold you up on the stage! All right, let's go through that scale again."

They went through it several times, and would have repeated it once more, but at this point, the pianist came in. She had a cup of coffee for Maestro. Jane looked at it with longing. While he sipped it, the accompanist dusted the ashes off the piano keys.

"Well, good, let's start with the recitative," the teacher said. "The introduction, please."

Renata played the opening bars. Jane sang the first note and was stopped abruptly.

"Never!" shouted Maestro, banging his score against the music stand. "Do you think you're singing for the D.A.R. in Virginia? That first note must be heard in the last balcony. Your first note establishes the whole opera. We'll start again."

They went through it ten times, the one note, until Maestro was satisfied. By this time his glasses were wet from being handled and pushed into place so often, and he had removed his coat, but even then he was perspiring. The pupil stood straight and determined.

"You got the volume that last time," was the closest Maestro came to a compliment. "Now we'll do it once more, for the diction."

The lesson raged on. Sometimes at a regular pause,

more often shouting above a passage, you could hear the teacher, "Open your mouth!"

"Stand straight!"

"Push your chin back!"

"Pronounce your words!"

"Smile!"

"SMILE!"

Then, if the pupil heard it once, she heard it a dozen times, "Don't pucker your lips!"

"Full, open tone, never let down, keep going!"

Jane was used to strenuous lessons, but this was one of the worst. She wondered what would give out first, her voice or her knees. Then she developed a tickling in her throat while sustaining a high note. She was certain she would choke to death, but she kept the note going while the tears ran down her cheeks.

"Brava, brava! It's better to cry in the studio than on the stage." A bit more gently he added, "All right, we'll let that go for this time. It'll do today, but tomorrow it must be richer and warmer. Singing, cara, is an emotion, not a mental exercise. You mustn't think so much. Let go! The school days are over. You're a prima donna now, so sing and act like one!"

He made a wide gesture and knocked over the music stand. Jane didn't even smile. She stood with her head high and her eyes sparkling. She really felt like banging him over the head, but she was determined not to lose control. While he was talking, lighting another cigarette and coughing, the telephone rang. As Maestro walked over to pick up the phone, Jane started to sit down. He motioned to her to get up.

"Work your arm exercises."

The pianist walked over to the window to try and get a little air. She didn't open it though.

Maestro was soon back, and the pianist scurried to the piano. The lesson went on and on. At last Jane sang an aria musically and emotionally to his satisfaction, then he stormed at her Italian, "If you're not going to work on your pronunciation, go home and sing American opera."

Finally the prima donna could take no more, and she threw down her music and swore loudly. Maestro stepped forward. The two musicians glared silently at each other. Finally the teacher said firmly, "That is the last time you swear in this studio or any place. The great artists learn control!"

He looked at his watch and smiled, "Per carita, we've gone way over our time. Let's go and have dinner. That will restore your good spirits!"

As Maestro was gathering together his music, he noticed a score, "Wait a minute, we haven't done *Norma*."

The lesson went on. Jane sang and sang, Maestro shouted and yelled, while the pianist was thankful she was not an opera singer.

"More fire, keep the motor going. Give, GIVE of yourself!" intoned the Maestro.

When the aria was over, no one said anything for a while. Finally the teacher reached out his hand and smiled, "That's the finest Italian singing you've done. Now let's go and eat!"

4
Do It Now

A few minutes later when the disheveled teacher and worn prima donna came into the dining room, Signora Rolandi greeted them warmly, "At last, here come the warriors! As soon as you're ready, we'll have dinner."

There was the fragrance of garlic, tomatoes and onions coming from the kitchen. "Italian perfume" as Jane called it. The singer had learned to appreciate Italian food and ate (that is, when Maestro would let her) with the same enthusiasm as she did everything else. She particularly enjoyed Signora's cooking.

Maestro had been a friend of the Rolandi family for years. Signora Rolandi's husband had been an important editor in Milan, and they had always had their home open to musicians and artists. Now that her husband was dead, Signora carried on the tradition. She had quickly developed an affection for Maestro's pupil, who was so unaffected and friendly. Signora had heard that she was from a distinguished old family in Virginia, and that her father was President of the Norfolk and Western Railroad, but Jane never boasted of these matters. She spoke only with warmth and tenderness about her family and friends in America.

After the singer had had her second serving of saltimbocca, and was obviously enjoying the salad,

Jane's mother said to her, "I can see clearly that when you come back to Milan in February you will be well taken care of!"

Maestro, again poised and smiling, said, "I promise you, Mrs. Smith, that we'll do everything possible to put your daughter on the best opera stages in the world, and at the same time watch over her too...."

"Maestro," Jane said with annoyance, as she held up her glass for Signora to fill again, "How do you expect me to be a prima donna when you insist upon treating me as a child?"

Maestro gently took the bottle from Signora and said, "A little wine is good for the voice, but another glass is bad." He went into one of his long lectures, "Cara, your parents have already spent a great deal of money on your career, several others of us have invested hours of our time and energy, and no matter what it costs you in the way of discipline, we're going to see that you do nothing to abuse your voice. I am training you to be a star, my dear, not third best or even second best!"

He went on. He spoke only to Jane, but the others at the table also fell under the spell of his words, "Think what it means to your family for you to become a famous singer, particularly your mother. She could have sung in opera with her voice and talent, but she chose to marry instead, and now she is willing to stand behind you as you rise in the opera world. Get it in your head, Salamona, you are not in this thing alone."

Maestro, who rarely drank anything stronger than coffee, took a sip of his seventh or eighth cup for the day, and concluded, "If you don't want to be a prima donna, cara, tell us now; it will save all of us time, energy and money."

Maestro had dark, penetrating eyes, and he gave his pupil one of the "looks" all his musicians knew well and which had such power over them.

Jane again experienced that mixed feeling. First she

33

wanted to knock down everyone for not letting her live her own life. Then she sighed, realizing that this was the way it must be. She *did* want to be a star, not only for the sake of others, but for herself too. She loved singing and acting and the thrill of being on stage, and she loved succeeding too. As she looked around the table at her mother, whom she loved deeply, and her two Italian friends who were so loyal to her, she made a deeper resolve that she would not let them down. All this time she had been holding the empty wine glass in her hand. Abruptly she placed it on the table and pushed it away.

That night before going to bed, Jane read through some of her notebooks. This included not only what she was learning in her voice lessons, but also advice scribbled down from many sources. She copied out on a special piece of paper to clip on her *Norma* score some advice given by Martha Graham, "Don't say I'll be able to do it in five years, and give over to waiting rather than trying!! Do it now."

This became the young opera singer's mental discipline for the next few years. The Maestro's strenuous demands she endeavored to carry out with as little murmuring as possible. No more wasting time. No more stanting still. If she intended to be a prima donna, and she intended to, it was now or never. When Jane and her mother left for the United States, the singer still had the "Do it now" reminder clipped to the music of *Norma*.

5
Eager to Work

"**I**'ve sent a few cables letting the newspapers in Roanoke know you're going to be home for a couple of weeks, cara, so when you get off the train, don't forget to smile," said Maestro as they swept into the busy Milan airport, with three porters arguing behind them over the pile of luggage, "and don't go out every night, although you must go out some and let people see you. Have several big cocktail parties, however, watch your diet; be captivating, and act as...."

Maestro didn't finish his thought as he was trying to see someone near the magazine stand, but Jane did, "Act as though opera was the most important thing in the world!"

"Yes!" whispered Maestro to Jane, not hearing what she was saying, "yes, there goes the music critic for the *Rome Roundup* into the coffee bar!"

He turned to Jane's mother and said, "Mrs. Smith, do you mind checking the tickets? It is important for Jane to meet Cassio. A good review from him can mean a lot to a young singer."

Quickly Maestro maneuvered Jane close to the music critic; however, he let him discover them first. After their embracing and allowing the critic time to notice the singer, Maestro presented his pupil.

Cassio was impressed with the appearance of the young star and spent some time telling her that. Finally he turned to Maestro. "Congratulations, my friend, you always work with the best. When do I have the privilege of hearing Miss Smith sing?"

"She is on her way to New York now and I follow in a month," Maestro explained. "We have many auditions, recordings, radio and TV appearances. She will be back in Nice early in February."

They stayed for several minutes, Jane, on the surface cool and charming, but inside in a turmoil wondering if her mother was able to check the tickets by herself and anxious about the time of departure.

At last Maestro looked at his watch. They didn't miss the plane, but there was a frantic moment before they boarded the large, trans-Atlantic jet and waved a farewell to Maestro and the music critic, who insisted upon coming to the gate with them.

Jane thoroughly disliked flying and usually took a couple of sleeping tablets just before a flight. But in the excitement of meeting the music critic she had forgotten her pills. Just before the plane took off she called the stewardess to bring a glass of water. Remembering Maestro's advice to show warmth to all people, Jane thanked the girl so graciously that all across the ocean she and her mother received that special attention reserved for special people.

When Jane swallowed her pills, she said to her mother, "Let's talk about opera until the sleeping tablets start working. I don't want to have to think about being in an airplane."

It was no effort for either of them to speak about opera, and the talk went on until they were far over the ocean. Mrs. Smith put into words what Jane was beginning to see for herself.

"You will soon have all the necessary materials to be a singer," her mother said, "but what must happen before your next important appearances is largely up to you."

Jane yawned comfortably. Her mother turned to see if she was going to sleep.

"Go on, go on," murmured the singer. "I'm listening."

"Well, I was saying, now it's up to you. You must figure out in your own mind how to make your experience and instruction your own. A singer is like a painter who has all the colors. A teacher can show you how to paint a picture, but in order to make it personal and have an inner glow, the artist has to find a special color or style of his own."

Jane nodded in agreement as she adjusted her pillow, still trying to go to sleep.

"For the time being I'm Turandot and Norma," she said, "but I can hardly wait to move to Wagner. Brunnhilde—that's my style!"

Finally Jane went to sleep, but not to leave opera behind. In her dream, Maestro was shouting, "Sing like a violin! Make a sound like a cello! a violin! a cello!" and she kept changing back and forth from a violin to a cello, singing above his shouting. When she woke up with a start, she realized that what she was hearing was the whine of the jets as they began the long descent to New York.

As quickly as they could after landing they transferred to the Pennsylvania Station and Jane felt as if she were already home when she saw the familiar and beloved Norfolk and Western train waiting to take them to Roanoke. The conductor was ready to help them and said, "We've been reading about you in the paper, Miss Smith. We're honored to have you come back home for a visit."

Another train official came up to say that Mr. Smith would be waiting on the platform for them. He also congratulated the singer.

37

Later in the day when the train crossed into Virginia, Jane shed quiet tears. You only have to go away from home for a while to know how much you love it. As they drew closer to Roanoke, Jane began to get excited about seeing her father, the rest of the family and many good friends. Some of the fun drained out of her expectation when she thought of all Maestro's orders and the fact that photographers would be there. She sighed as she put on fresh makeup and polished her shoes by rubbing them on the back of her stockings.

As the train slowed down, she quickly saw her father. Her mother had glimpsed him too. Together they watched him help a short, older lady put her heavy suitcase on an outgoing train across the platform. Soon he melted into the group again, smiling and talking to this person and that.

Jane wanted to jump off the train and rush into her father's arms, but years of training restrained her. Maestro would have been proud of his young star could he have seen her come down the train steps. She moved evenly and gracefully, and when the photographers saw her, she gave them a lovely smile. As she spoke with a reporter about her performance in Venice, she was effervescent, but modest.

Her father stood at the back of the crowd surrounding the singer. There was a look of gentle amusement upon his face. Perhaps he was remembering what seemed only a few years ago, the same daughter, his youngest child, galloping and shouting in her special cowboy outfit with her brothers teasing her, "Here comes the fat cowboy!"

Jane's visit home was a happy, exciting time, and for a short while she forgot all about the training, her la k of freedom and the other demanding parts of opera life. She had no difficulty carrying out Maestro's orders to "get out and be seen, go to a few parties, let the people know you're in town!"

Before Jane stepped into her home the telephone started ringing for her, and the whirl of dinners, interviews and parties began almost immediately and continued throughout her visit. She was asked to sing on several occasions, but she refused politely. It was another of Maestro's injunctions, "Don't spread yourself out thinly. You are a professional singer now. People don't ask a dentist at a dinner party to examine their teeth, do they? Well, they shouldn't ask a singer to sing. Learn to say no, or you will have no voice for the stage."

Jane enjoyed her Virginia holiday, and it was intoxicating to be treated as a star, but when it was time to go to New York, she was glad. A person accustomed to working hard needs only short vacations. She was eager to work again, to pick up where she had left off.

6
Learning to Walk

In Jane's former years in New York City, she was still the lighthearted school girl enjoying freedom and dreaming about being an opera star. She was never at rest. Her life was a perpetual going, doing, seeing, learning. She lived at the Three Arts Club, and to save money she walked the thirty-seven blocks to Juilliard every day. More than one person turned to take a second glance at the lively, laughing Southerner either reciting Milton's *Allegro* to improve her diction, or reviewing the gestures in an opera role.

Then she had languages to work on, not only Italian, French and German, but English. When Maestro first heard her Southern accent, he exclaimed, "Young lady, I cannot understand you, and neither will your audiences. I'm sure it's charming, but that accent will have to go!"

Jane never had a weight problem in New York, because she spent most of her food allowance on concerts, theater tickets, movies, books and records.

"After a greasy cup of soup and some stale crackers," she recorded in her diary, "we went in the pouring rain to *Fantasia*. My fourth time, and it's still great, but I've just got to catch up on sleep."

"Reading *Pickwick Papers*. Really tickles me when

Dickens describes these men and their troubles. Must remember to get all of Dickens' works; he's a wonderful writer. Had a thin hamburger for supper, and then went to the concert...."

Another day she recorded, "Only had twenty-five cents for lunch today. Drove the waitress crazy asking the price of everything. Plan to hear Eileen Farrell tonight. Bought wonderful recording of Norma."

And the next day, "Just finished a burnt hot dog, back to practicing. The movie last night was impossible. Wish I had stayed home and read Dickens."

And another, "After a fair supper, more Schubert. I'll sing all fifty songs in that book this winter...."

And she did.

Jane never did things halfheartedly. If she started something, she went all the way. But being a student in New York City did not mean she was always lighthearted. More than once she recorded in her diary, "My usual depressed self on Monday."

"Words not good yet, too much pretty singing. Must learn to 'give' in the theater, no inhibitions...."

"I detest my shyness. It makes me seem stiff and unfriendly. My singing lacks excitement and life!"

"In terrible voice today. Must never exercise before a lesson."

"Wonder what I'm doing here spending my father's money. I don't seem to be getting any place, so much red tape to make a singer."

Then a few days later, she wrote, "All I have to offer is youth and an eager mind."

It was in these early student days that the "eager mind" resolved to read all of the classics listed in the Modern Library. Being orderly, as well as eager, she bought them one at a time, beginning with Henry Adams, and by 1951 she was deep in Marcel Proust. The Dickens' days were over...

Jane's routine in New York City was nearly the same as in Italy, but there were no Milanese dinners served by Signora Rolandi to help recover her spirit after a lesson with Maestro. But something had changed with the singer since her visit home and the growing awareness of her responsibility to an entire city to be successful. She complained less and less. The louder Maestro shouted, the more serene and statuesque she became, "Stick tongue out and pull face long, at the same time push from stomach." Dutifully the tongue would shoot out until she could almost touch the tip of her nose with her tongue, and her stomach muscles became as hard as a fighter's. Still Maestro prodded her, "breathing bad—never breathe with shoulders. Breathe with the whole chest."

Finally when the breathing was mastered, he started on something else, "You must get contact lenses. You can't wander around the stage in a fog. It's imperative to see every move of conductor and prompter. Put your glasses back on and look into the mirror as you sing that phrase again. Your face should always look pretty when singing. Never, never have a strained expression. It's a sign of poor training and technique...."

After each lesson the singer would go back to her room and write down everything the teacher said. By now she had utmost confidence in him and wanted to be able to go over and over the things he taught her. What Maestro knew about the theater and what the audience is seeking in the singers was inexhaustible. He had been in opera since he was nine years old and sang in children's opera. Almost from the beginning of his musical career he wanted to be a voice teacher, and after years of preparation, training and successful appearances as a singer, he was ready to teach, and what made his teaching special was his personal concern for his pupils. He loved them as if they were his own children, and they, in turn, became devoted to him and learned to accept the fireworks and bombast of his teaching as a normal part of a lesson.

"Don't dance around so much," he complained one day. "Think of the people who are watching you. You're a large person, cara, but it's no handicap on the opera stage. It's a tremendous asset, *if* you learn to move gracefully. Princess Turandot—well, remember, she's a *Princess*!! She mustn't come striding out on stage like a cowhand or in a slow, lazy Southern walk!"

Jane winced, but said nothing. He continued, "Be relaxed! Relaxed!! Do you hear me?"

The pupil heard him all right. That night when she was having supper with a friend who was a modern dancer, she said, "Lucy, I've got to learn to walk. Maestro said some horrid things today," she paused, and added grimly, "but I'm afraid he's right. You don't suppose you can help me?"

The dancer got up lightly from the table and crossed the room to get the telephone book. They had talked of this problem before, but had never really done anything about it.

Jane sighed as she watched her friend move, "What a shame you can't sing! That's the way Maestro wants *me* to walk. He says I stride on the stage as if I were a cowboy!"

Jane groaned and Lucy laughed as she thumbed through the pages. Before she dialed, Lucy said seriously, "The point is, you can sing, and I know one person in New York who will convince you that you *are* a Princess when she gets through with you—Martha Graham."

"*Martha Graham!* Lucy, are you out of your mind? She only works with the best! She'll die when she sees me in a leotard, and so will I! No, no, no ... I couldn't possibly ... can't you give me some exercises?"

Lucy looked hard at Jane, "Miss Graham is a very intelligent lady. She respects artists with determination. You two will get along fine. I'll explain the situation to her."

And that is how the singer came to study dance with Martha Graham. As she explained to Lucy when they met again, "I was right on the front row, and I felt like a waltzing elephant, but I'm sticking. It's already helped. Maestro hasn't called me a cowhand in weeks!"

And so the disciplined routine of the young singer went on and on. Usually she had her lights out by ten thirty (Maestro's orders), but that did not mean she always went right to sleep. Many nights she would review in her mind the things she was learning. Sometimes she would recall her marvelous years at Stuart Hall and Hollins College. Other times, if she was discouraged, her mind would explore what was the point in all this struggle to become someone.

Often Jane wrestled with the problem of the meaning of life. She wondered too why she always had to have an undercurrent of dissatisfaction, but, perhaps, as Martha Graham had said recently, it was a good sign to be never satisfied. But this bothered Jane. She turned on her bed light and reached for her notebook to read what Miss Graham had said, "No artist is pleased. There is no satisfaction whatever at any time. There is only a queer divine dissatisfaction, a blessed unrest that keeps us marching and makes us more alive than the others."

Jane shook her head and said to herself, "I don't think that is right. There must be a place of rest in life even for the artist. I believe I'd really come alive if I could get rid of my unrest."

It took the singer a long time to go to sleep that night but in the morning, after a strong cup of black coffee, she was ready to go again, and the restless thoughts of the night had passed from her mind as if they had been part of a dream.

Around Christmas she wrote to her parents,

44

"Maestro's teaching is the most thorough and intensive I've ever been subjected to, and, bless his heart, he is achieving his goal, even though on occasions he makes me so MAD I could scream! But he is beginning to make me want to do everything more carefully.... I honestly look forward to singing in Nice. I feel ready."

7
Technique and Art

"**W**hat confusion!" Jane remarked to her mother. She had just returned from her first rehearsal of *Turandot* in Nice. "The members of the chorus and orchestra understand only French, and the conductor is shouting at them in Italian." She laughed, "There's more drama in rehearsals than in the operas themselves."

Jane was sitting with her feet up on another chair, trying to be as comfortable as possible while enjoying the warmth. She had the door to the dressing room open, and the Mediterranean sun was streaming in. Her mother was sitting by the dressing table sewing more sequins and jewels on a costume. She asked, "Did you sing in a full voice?"

"I certainly did, and I was the only one too." She added with determination. "Maestro is right. When you hold back during a rehearsal, it carries over into the performance."

Mrs. Smith handed Jane a bottle, "Here, take a couple more of these vitamins. What a pity you have a cold, but small wonder. It gets so cold here at night."

Jane swallowed the pills and took a few of her own. Then she smeared more Vicks on her neck and chest.

"Just before he kissed me in the last scene, Luccioni whispered, 'You smell like a pharmacy!' " Jane laughed and her mother joined in too, but added soberly,

"I hope you don't infect the whole company."

"They'll tar and feather me if I do. Any singer hates singing with a cold! It's the worst thing that can happen, and then I can't hear." The singer hit against the side of her head hoping to loosen the congestion. "I'm thankful to Maestro for insisting that I never skip a lesson simply because I wasn't well." She sighed, "I've had him yelling at me when I felt worse than this, so I guess I'll get through the performance."

The following night when they arrived back at the beautiful opera house for the first performance, Jane remembered to bring along autographed pictures of herself to give to the doorman, the maid, the stagehands and several in the chorus who had asked her. It had taken Jane years to get where she was; she, better than anyone, knew the work involved, the things she had sacrificed, but now that she was beginning to be noticed and respected as a star, it all seemed unreal to her, as if she were handing out autographed pictures of someone else.

Later in the evening when she sustained the difficult high notes demanded of the Princess Turandot and raged about the stage ordering heads cut off here and there, no one in the delighted audience knew that the leading lady was singing under a handicap. The morning papers gave her excellent reviews with the exception of one small observation by a columnist who said that he thought Miss Smith looked more like a "Walküre" than a petite Chinese Princess. As Jane wrote to Maestro when she sent him the reviews, "I'd like to see a cute, little thing sing Turandot! These critics and their foolish remarks! Obviously he has never sung a note himself, why...." And much more.

Maestro answered sympathetically, "The overall reviews were grand. You didn't even mention that, but you are right, cara, Puccini wrote the music for *Turandot* for a big dramatic voice, and, as all musicians know, a large voice needs a large case. A cello doesn't come in a piccolo frame!"

Jane's teacher, even in his letter, did not let his singer sit back and enjoy her success very long. "The Nice performances are over. I'm proud of you, and now we go on. It probably won't be the last time you sing on stage with a cold and fever. My friend, Riccio, the baritone, who had a wonderfully successful career, told me once that he could remember only a handful of performances when he had felt really good. No one ever knew it. He sang brilliantly, and the secret is technique and art! It is never enough for an artist to have only a great voice. If you learn nothing else from me, you're going to learn technique and art...."

In the early part of March when Jane and her mother arrived in the music-loving city of Palermo, they were both awed when they saw the beautiful Massimo Theater, and scarcely had to be told by the impresario, "This is the largest stage in Europe!"

Almost immediately the rehearsals began, and if Jane did not sing in one, she attended the others in order to keep learning, even if it meant turning down several tempting invitations. She did go to a couple of parties, one of them was in a palace outside the city, but she ate and drank little and went home early.

At the opening performance, in the moments shortly before the curtain was to rise, Jane discovered with horror that she had left her contact lenses across town at the hotel where they were staying. Without being told her mother rushed out of the room, ran down the long staircase of the theater, and without knowing a word of Italian, she ordered a taxi to go full speed to the Hotel delle Palme. With wild gestures and sheer willpower she communicated to the driver that she would be right back as soon as she found something in her room. In a few minutes she returned victoriously with the contact lenses, and she and her driver, who was by this time enjoying the drama, flew back across town in time for the show to go on.

It was this characteristic of persistence in Jane's mother that was the ultimate secret behind Jane's career. Many singers have excellent voices, the right teaching and contacts, and are willing to work hard themselves, but even then they sing in a few performances and are never heard of again. It takes something else to be successful in opera, and Mrs. Smith had that. Her determination to go through, to go on, in spite of obstacles, was amazing, often amusing, and nearly always successful.

When Jane made her curtain calls at the last performance amid "bravas" and stamping feet, she not only acknowledged the applause of the front rows and lower balconies, but she looked all the way to the top balcony. It was a wonderful sight to see the smiling faces, the bouquets of real flowers edging each balcony, the elegance of the opera house. She could not remember a more exciting moment.

8
"She Belongs to Us"

When Jane arrived in Roanoke in October 1952, to make her American concert debut, the people of her home town were eagerly waiting for the special event. She was already well-known because of her years at Hollins College as a soloist, and also because of the prominence of her family. But now Jane was returning home after several very successful appearances in Europe as an opera singer. One of her friends said this, "You must remember that many of us in Virginia had been following Jane's career long before she became an opera star. Besides being the soloist for the Hollins choir, we often heard her on the radio. When she made her opera debut in Detroit, many of us went to hear her. We would have been in Venice, Nice and Sicily too, if we could have, but few of us have missed much. I have a whole scrapbook of clippings about Jane. The Virginia newspapers have been proud of her too."

And not only the Virginia papers. Her name was beginning to appear around the world. In the Rome *Daily American* on the front page, it was reported, "Jane Stuart Smith, statuesque American soprano who has scored dramatic success in the title role of Puccini's *Turandot*, will return to the U.S. next month for her first concert tour in her native land...."

From Palermo the newspaper *Sicilia del Popolo* had just reported, "The beautiful and cruel Turandot was brought to life by Jane Stuart Smith, with a voice which is fresh, flexible and perfectly schooled ... with acting which was convincing, poised and distinguished."

A society editor in the Los Angeles *Express* said, "Jane Stuart Smith, the pretty Roanoke, Virginia, girl who caused quite a flurry among the titled set in Venice, has been signed to open the winter season in Palermo."

In the New York *Post* Leonard Lyons ran this item, "Salvador Dali has been in Venice these past few days. In San Marco Square he met Jane Stuart Smith, the opera singer, who went there to sing *Turandot*. She noticed that Dali was wearing a pink phosphorescent shirt and gloves. 'Why?' she asked him ... 'This is my answer,' said Dali, 'to Italy's weak electricity system.' "

The October concert was "unforgettable," said a Roanoke music critic. "When Jane came out on the stage, the entire audience stood up and cheered and applauded, even before she sang! I had never seen that. Then at the intermission she was nearly buried in flowers. It was the most exciting concert I've been to. I don't remember now how many encores there were. At the end Jane thanked the audience in a charming and modest way and the clapping started again!"

And as Mrs. Natalie Small, who was a key person in arranging the concert, wrote for the programs, "We are very proud of Jane ... proud of her achievements ... proud that we can call her ours ... and especially proud that her concert debut is in her home city, Roanoke. While we will always feel she belongs to us, we will gladly share and wish for her the best of fortune as she sings before the appreciative audiences throughout our country."

Many people dream of returning one day in triumph to their home towns. Jane Stuart Smith was one of the few who did. On the editorial page of the Roanoke *Times* came this tribute (usually reserved for the dead), "Roanoke has a number of sons and daughters who have won fame and fortune in various fields. In none does the city take greater pride and interest than in Jane Stuart Smith...." Quoting only these few publicity notices from hundreds of them, it helps to explain the anguish in her heart, seven years later, when she felt certain it was the Lord's will for her to leave the opera world. But this is going ahead of the story....

From her brilliant appearance in Roanoke Jane went to Carnegie Hall. Soon after, she was asked to sing on the Railroad Hour. This was followed by a concert in Albany, New York. In between times she continued her practice, study and lessons, as well as appearing on TV, singing for auditions and interviews.

In the summer of 1954 the singer flew back to Italy to prepare for several operas and a concert tour the following year. And in August she signed her largest contract—to sing in the Royal Opera House of Cairo, Egypt, ten performances in all. The Virginian was on her way.

9
Down in Egypt

Professionally Jane grew in confidence during the years 1952-54 which liberated her voice (success is a great thing for a young singer if rightly applied), but her inward, personal battles did not lessen. She had long ceased trying to discuss with her friends the moral and spiritual issues which troubled her, as these conversations always ended unsatisfactorily.

"Stop reading so much!" one of the tenors with whom she was working told her. "All religions are the same, so why bother studying them; they're just sweet pills for those who don't have guts to live."

"You call this living?" Jane fired back. "Why, every moment of our lives is make-believe and ordered. We don't have any time to think for ourselves. Maybe we're afraid to think. That's it, I think we're afraid to think, and that's why I love to read. It makes me think."

Dino watched the singer with an amused expression, "What is it you are thinking *this* time?"

"All right, for a starter, I want to know what comes later. True, things are going well for us today, but I'm from a railroad family where you learn to think ahead. What I want to know is what's going to happen when I'm old and no longer have a stage to walk on and fans to applaud me and...."

Dino tried to put his arm around the singer, but she quickly stepped back and continued talking. "I'm sure I love opera as much as you do—at least I work harder," (the tenor's large stomach was evidence he did not train strictly!) "but all I'm saying is I think there's more to life than this. Doesn't it ever bother you, wondering what's at the end? At the best, you've probably got another ten years on the stage." (He winced, but the grin never left his face.) In exasperation, Jane exclaimed, "Don't you ever wonder about the purpose of it all, Dino? Why we're here, where we're going, and what...."

Finally he took hold of her and firmly put his hand over her mouth and laughed loudly, "No, NO! my dear, I never make it my business to think more than one meal ahead! Which reminds me, let's have lunch."

Jane learned to wrestle with her problems alone, while walking in the park, while flying to performances, while roaming through a museum, even when standing in the wing of a theater, waiting to make her entrance on stage. She had an active, deep mind and was able to think and act on different levels.

As the time approached for her to sing in Egypt, she felt ready musically and technically, but she could not rid herself of the depression which had fastened on to her. The weather in Milan did not help. For weeks the big, teeming city had been blanketed under a chilling fog. There was no place to get warm, but what bothered Jane more was the inner, chilling struggle going on in her soul. She kept asking herself, "What's wrong with me? There are hundreds of singers in Milan who would give anything to be standing in my shoes. I should be thankful and grateful and overjoyed for the success I've already had, but what is this empty feeling which is nagging me? Perhaps Dino is right, I shouldn't think so much."

Jane had included the Bible in her constant reading.

In fact, wherever she travelled she carried the copy given to her by her parents when she attended Stuart Hall, and she read it with the same critical spirit of questioning she applied to all her reading. She had received most of her religious training from professors who considered the Bible a book of myths, so she too had little respect for the truth of the Scriptures.

On the night before she left for Cairo she said her usual evening prayer, the repeating of the Lord's Prayer. In the midst of her words, suddenly she thought, if there is a real God, it would seem that I could say more to Him and get beyond the ceiling of this room.

In the excitement of getting to the airport the next day, Jane recovered her enthusiasm, and as the plane lifted into the air, she was awed to think she was actually on the way to the mysterious land of history and ancient culture. Jane loved traveling, and as this was the first time she had had the opportunity to go to Egypt, she was nearly as thrilled about seeing the land with the mighty past as singing there.

Several hours later when the plane circled the immense city of Cairo and Jane saw the gleaming Nile River in the desert moonlight, she gasped at the beauty of the scene viewed from that height; and in a few moments when she picked her way through the press of people in the dimly lighted building which served as an airport, immediately she felt the darkness of Egypt and wondered what was ahead.

When two others in the opera company and herself finally found a taxi, they were met with the same confusing, noisy mob of people, and mostly men and children, Jane observed. They were dressed poorly and many barefooted. Those who were fairly well-dressed were wearing tall, red hats with black tassels. In some of the narrow streets the driver could scarcely get through the waves of people. She was shocked when she saw some of the men up close, and they were bold about looking into the taxi windows; many had eye diseases and sores on their faces, and there seemed to be no relief from the bad smell she had first noticed at the airport.

Jane made two comments in her notebook after her first drive through Cairo, "I'd be running in the streets too if I had to live the way many do in Cairo."

"I'm no longer sure that all religions are the same; certainly the end results are not the same."

The musicians began to wonder what their living accommodation would be like, and if they would ever be able to put out of their minds their first impression of Egypt, but then the driver turned a corner and they were immediately in another world. Many of the buildings were modern and new on either side of a wide boulevard. After a short drive they spun around a traffic circle with a fountain in the center and surrounded by a formal garden and the driver pointed out the beautiful Royal Opera House, and down the street to the large hotel where Jane was to stay. The other members of the opera company were staying in a pension a few blocks from the theater. Jane was tempted to go along with the others, because the thought of being alone in this strange, foreboding city was frightening, but Maestro had made the reservation and it was his idea that she always stay in the best hotels in the cities where she sang. "A first-class singer must present a first-class image," he would say.

The rehearsals were to start the next morning, so after Jane registered and unpacked her suitcases she went to bed. Her first few days in Egypt she worked diligently and went to bed early each night. But the third day she broke the "training rules" and went to a luncheon party in a magnificent villa outside Cairo, and later in the day she and the other guests were taken to see the pyramids. Jane wrote in her diary, "My first

56

ride on a camel and as we were returning to the pyramids we saw the sun set in an amazing sweep of purple, pink and red over the mysterious and vast Sahara desert."

Jane had looked forward to getting out of the city for the afternoon, but she was dismayed to see that many of the country people were as poor as the city dwellers. They lived in miserable, small, mud huts built below the dusty roads which were built up high. The thought of staying in Egypt two months was dreadful. "If only I had brought more books with me to read," Jane thought, but then it all changed after the first performance.

The Egyptian maid told her that she had an important visitor waiting to see her at the stage door. Normally Jane did not allow anyone in her dressing room after a strenuous performance as she needed time to recover her strength, but the little maid was so excited and tried to explain to Jane that her visitor was a famous hero in Egypt, and so mostly to please the girl, Jane told her to invite in "the hero."

10
Worlds Apart

"The hero" was not what Jane expected. Modestly and quietly he explained that he was a journalist and would like to interview her for his paper. He said a few right words about her performance and began asking the singer questions. Soon they were talking comfortably. The maid (who was now sitting in the far corner of the dressingroom looking with adoring eyes at the noble Egyptian) had tried to explain to her mistress that the reason Kamal was a hero was that he had recently discovered the sun boats near the Giza pyramid. Jane asked him about his archaeological discovery. She had remembered reading about the sun boats in *Time* magazine.

Kamal said, "The best thing is to see them."

He smiled, "If you can arrange some free time tomorrow in the afternoon, I would enjoy showing them to you."

Jane said that she would be delighted to go.

On the following day, Kamal sent his chauffeur and car to pick up the opera singer at three in the afternoon, and during the next two months, the doorkeeper at the hotel where Jane was staying grew accustomed to seeing the fair, attractive American and the dark, handsome Egyptian come and go together, sometimes in the afternoons, more often at night when Jane did not have a performance. As he said to the head waiter one day while he watched them walk in the direction of the theater, "Those two surely have a lot to talk about. My wife hasn't said as much to me in all the years we've been married as Miss Smith has said to Mr. Kamal these past few weeks! They like each other!"

Maestro would have been furious had he known the hours his singer kept in Cairo, but suddenly, there was so much to do and see in and around the city, and Kamal was such good company, and....

Her performances did not suffer from the breaking of the rules, because Jane did rest the days before she appeared on stage, but some of the rehearsals were not as pleasant. The conductor was an irritable man, but Jane had to admit her tiredness made her edgy too. They had a few disagreements which upset the singer, but then Kamal would call for her, and soon they would be laughing together and she would forget her irritation and tiredness.

The Egyptian was not only a writer, poet and an archaeologist, but a philosopher, and he enjoyed talking to Jane. He didn't laugh at her questions. They discussed religion for hours. Kamal was not a Moslem. He belonged to the Coptic Church, which is an ancient branch of the Christian religion, but as far as understanding the authentic Christian faith, his comprehension was not any better than the singer's.

"If Buddha has something wise to say to me today," Kamal said smiling, "I listen. Perhaps tonight it will be Confucius, the Apostle Paul or Benjamin Franklin. I believe in having an open mind to wisdom."

Kamal had engaged a boat for the afternoon. Jane enjoyed the rides on the Nile as much as anything they did in Egypt. It was always cool, and it was one place she felt free from the poverty and heaviness of the city. There was even something sinister about her hotel. Day and night a guard sat at the end of her corridor. They never exchanged a word, but he would watch her every move from the moment she stepped off the elevator and unlocked her door and entered her room. These were days of political turmoil in Egypt, and Jane felt uneasy almost all the time she was in Cairo, except when she was with Kamal.

"You mentioned the Apostle Paul," Jane said. "What do you think of the Bible, Kamal?"

"As literature it is unexcelled, particularly the style.... Translations do not mar it. The Bible has a beautiful style in all languages, and...."

"I'm thinking more about the miracles. Can we in the twentieth century believe in a supernatural God? I hardly think so."

Kamal said, "I think of the miracles as props to help illustrate the Biblical stories. They don't necessarily have to be true."

"Yes, that is what I have been taught too, but, Kamal, don't you ever wish they might be true? For example, Abraham. He has always bothered me. I don't like the way he 'bargained' with God, and I am particularly troubled at his willingness to sacrifice his own beloved son, but, on the other hand," she added wistfully, "wouldn't it be wonderful to know God as well as Abraham seemed to? I can't tell you where it is, but some place in the Bible it speaks of Abraham as the friend of God! Isn't that amazing?"

After their ride on the Nile Kamal took Jane to a private club where she met some of his friends, who were the intellectuals and nobility of Cairo. At first she was enchanted with the brilliant conversations, but not for long. After a while the words seemed brittle and empty. It bothered her how unrealistic these people were. It was the same thing that annoyed her in the theater, and it made her wonder if she would ever meet genuine people with intelligence, life and love of beauty. Kamal, yes, was different from his sophisticated friends, but he too lacked realism. He was not overly distressed by the poverty of most of his countrymen. It was taken for granted. It made Jane homesick for America. She wept that night when she thought seriously about what her own country did stand for. It is the land of opportunity, a free country. These are not trite words. "If my father had been born in Egypt," she thought, "I wouldn't have the liberty I have. What opportunity would he have had in Egypt?" (Jane's father had lost both of his parents when he was a boy. He was brought up by relatives on a Colorado ranch. All his life he had to work hard, and he enjoyed hard work, and it led to something.) Jane thought, "Many of these Egyptians work hard too, but where does it get them? What makes it this way? What is the difference?" When she drifted into sleep, Jane said to herself, "The difference must be God...."

One night towards the end of her stay in Egypt, Kamal came to Jane's dressing room after her next to last performance. He hadn't missed one. He loved music and he deeply appreciated her singing. Jane marveled that she sang as well as she did with the little sleep she had had in the past few weeks, and the emotional and mental strain she was experiencing.

"I was just speaking with the daughter of Puccini," Kamal said. Jane looked puzzled. "Yes," he said, "she heard you sing tonight," and Kamal, who always said the right thing to the singer added, "and she said that you sang Turandot the way her father would have wanted it!"

Jane looked at Kamal with tenderness, "That's the finest compliment I have ever received. Thank you, Kamal."

"She said, also, that she hoped she could meet you before you leave Cairo. She understood perfectly why you do not like to receive visitors after a performance."

While Jane changed into evening clothes, Kamal went back out to speak with friends. When the singer was ready, they went directly to a night club where he had arranged a party for the leading lady, so some visitors on a diplomatic trip from Washington could meet her. She talked to them with joy, because they represented home.

Later in the evening, Kamal and Jane stopped by at friends who lived in a modern apartment overlooking the Nile. The two young couples sat on the penthouse terrance talking about a book they had all read, Moravia's *The Conformist*. Jane tried to express to the others the feeling of despair and hopelessness she had when the story of suffering and agony ended on a note of shattering stillness, as if there was no reason, no purpose for life.

"Oh, there are reasons enough to live," her host said sarcastically. "Look how happy we are! We lack nothing. Nothing!" He looked to see if anyone needed refills, then poured himself a half of a glass of Scotch and drank it straight. Jane's eyes turned to the opposite shore of the Nile where under the deceptive shadow crouched filth, poverty and crime....

When Kamal accompanied her into the lobby of her hotel early in the morning, she knew it was the last time she would see him. There was an ache in her heart. She liked and admired the gentle, noble Egyptian, and possibly she loved him, though she never dared explore the thought deeply, because she knew they were worlds apart.

When two days later the plane lifted the singer above Cairo, and again she saw the Nile from the air, finally she made a giant step nearer to finding the answer to her emptiness, though at the time she did not know how important it was. As she looked at the desert below her and the vastness of the unending sky above, she cried out, "If there is a living God, show me!"

Jane was not sure to Whom she had addressed her question, and years later, she said, "I cannot explain it, but I knew in my heart I had been heard."

11
Feathers in Her Hat

As Jane looked at the ceiling of her hotel room (she was lying flat on her back in bed), she was smiling. I should be crying, she thought, but there is no point. The show must go on, it will go on.

What a chain of events since her arrival in Cincinnati to sing in the summer opera in the popular Zoological Garden. It seemed years ago when she said goodbye to Kamal in Cairo, rode a camel in the desert, walked on Mars Hill in Greece when she visited Athens on her way back to Milan, and hurriedly climbed through the catacombs of Rome on the same trip; and yet it was only a few months ago. The ringing of the telephone interrupted her thoughts.

"I'll answer it," she called to her maid, who was pressing Jane's dress in the other room. The telephone was conveniently located on the bed table, so Jane did not have to change her position to answer it. "Yes, yes," she told the hotel manager. "Send him up, but only the reporter, not the photographer. I don't believe the public would believe that I am planning to sing Friday night if they saw a picture of me in bed!"

A few minutes later when the reporter was seated at the bedside of the opera singer, he apologized for bothering her.

"No," Jane said sincerely, "I'm the one who is sorry. It is not my custom to break appointments, Mr. Gordon. I felt badly about keeping you waiting the other day, but when you hear perhaps you'll forgive me."

"You better start at the beginning," he said, "if you don't mind. The hotel manager told me that you had injured your back, but I'd rather get the story straight from you."

Jane explained, "As you know, costumes are an important part of a singer's life, and it is hard on them traveling back and forth across the ocean; so the other morning at the theater I was going through one of my trunks to see what might have to be mended. As I looked at the bottom of the trunk, I saw my headdress, but no feathers.

"In alarm, I started reaching, trying to find the plumes, and I guess I stretched too far and did something to my back." Jane winced at the memory, "It was dreadful. I was doubled up with pain and taken back to the hotel and a doctor was called. I've been here ever since. I missed the appointment with you, had to cancel an interview last night, plus a couple of rehearsals. The doctor gave me something for pain, and yesterday fitted me with a steel brace, so I plan to rehearse tomorrow, and, of course, sing on Friday."

"What a tough break," the reporter said kindly, "I'll try not to take too much time."

"That's all right," replied the singer, with a smile. "You know our motto, 'The show goes on.' "

"What's the inside story on the peacock feathers?"

Jane laughed, "The version you probably heard about my mother running about the zoo after peacocks is fiction, but it *is* true that I have a very determined mother, and as she takes pride in my costumes, she did not take the loss of the ostrich plumes lightly. Her immediate thought was how to replace them. Word got around and someone from the zoo actually did bring her a handful of peacock feathers, but she was determined to find ostrich plumes; and that is where she is right now, riding around town with a relative trying to find ostrich plumes!"

The reporter said, "I like the sound of your mother, and I imagine that she has had a lot to do with your successful career."

Jane nodded the best she could in her position, "She and my Maestro are the two reasons I am singing opera today. I never could have made it by myself."

The conversation was interrupted when Mrs. Smith and Jane's cousin burst into the room proudly waving ostrich plumes.

"Where did you get them?" Jane asked.

"It wasn't easy," her mother said, "but we finally heard of a wholesale house where they had everything. We got there just as it was about to close. Well, here they are!" she said, smiling, "exactly like the ones that got left behind in Italy."

"I used to think being a reporter was exciting," said Mr. Gordon grinning, "but it's tiresome compared to opera life. Thanks for the story, Jane Smith. Incidentally, I find your name and yourself refreshing among the hard-to-pronounce, hard-to-approach stars usually found on an opera bill. I'll be out to hear you Friday night and look forward to watching and hearing you in action!"

Jane did sing in Cincinnati with the steel brace on her back and new ostrich plumes in her headpiece. The famous outdoor theater is located near the zoo, and the night of the performance was one of Ohio's hottest, which made the animals in their cage restless. Every once in a while the opera singer said she heard the lions roar, but they must have made very loud sounds to get above the voice of Princess Turandot.

The reporter did attend the performance, as he said he would, and he thoroughly enjoyed the opera, particularly the singing of the leading lady, and he gave her a wonderful review in the morning paper.

Jane had a little less than a week at home in Virginia, and then she was back in an airplane returning to Europe. She wrote in her diary, "I want to learn the three Brunnhildes well this year and must find a German with whom to study. Haven't found an Italian conductor yet who knows anything about Wagner. Maestro will find someone for me though."

12
Same Old Problem

By August, Jane, with ostrich plumes and steel brace, was back in Europe auditioning in Salzburg before Karl Böhm and Rudolph Bing. The singer noted in her diary, "Really a good audition. Voice in wonderful form. Perhaps the weather and atmosphere, and the mountain air had something to do with it. Bing said, 'That's a beautiful voice.' "

On the same trip she auditioned as well as heard several Wagner operas at Bayreuth. One of the tenors showed Jane around the famous theater that was built as a memorial to Wagner. He also let her use his dressing room to rest in before her audition. The future Brunnhilde wrote only eight words about this visit, "The thrill of a lifetime to visit here."

But when she returned to Milan, a depression plagued her. She could not understand why she felt unhappy, but, in a sense, it was the same old problem Jane had been struggling with most of her adult life. During the months and years the singer spent in Milan, she fairly regularly attended church. If you asked her why she went, she would shrug her shoulders and say, "I guess it's because we have always gone to church in my family, and I would sort of miss it if I didn't go."

And so it was in this confused and unhappy frame of

mind that she went to the English-speaking church one grey Sunday morning. She sat in the back row and during the prayer she had a sudden surge of hope that maybe this would be the day she would make a discovery which would lift the depression from her. She leaned forward during the sermon straining to find meaning in the message for her life. But there was nothing there. The words of the vicar were as empty as the Egyptian intellectuals in Cairo.

During the singing of the last hymn, tears rolled down the face of the singer as she thought, "I'll never find the way. Probably there are no answers."

She left the service before it was finished, because she did not want to talk to anyone, but on the steps outside the church she heard someone call her, "Excuse me, you are Jane Stuart Smith?"

The speaker was a tiny wisp of a girl. Jane was thankful she had a hat with a veil. She couldn't stand to have anyone see that she had been crying. The small stranger spoke hurriedly, as if she were afraid the opera star would walk away before she could say all she wanted to say. "I've heard you sing several times, and I think you have a marvelous talent." She ran on breathlessly, "I study voice too, so I know what I'm saying...."

Jane was at first annoyed at the intrusion of her privacy, but her admirer's naive sincerity warmed her heart, and she replied kindly, "Thank you, that's good of you to say so."

Abruptly, the small one asked, "Could I invite you to dinner?"

Jane was in no mood to talk to anyone, let alone a stranger. As graciously as she could she thanked her, but explained it was impossible. The girl looked so disappointed, Jane added quickly, "Perhaps I can come another time."

Jane reached in her pocketbook and found a calling

card, "Here's my telephone number, you can call me."

Jane handed her the card, said she was glad to have met her, they shook hands and parted. Jane was glad to get away from the persistent one, and yet she had a feeling it was more than chance their meeting on the church steps. She found herself humming Wagner's theme of destiny. She felt it had something to do with a letter she had received the day before from her Aunt Emma. Normally her aunt's letters were full of family news and cheerful, but all this note said was that it is darkest before the dawn. It was a puzzle to Jane how her aunt knew she was in a troubled state.

Aunt Emma was a favorite in Jane's family. She had certain "extreme" ideas about religion, even would speak about "talking with the Lord," but her relatives excused her religious enthusiasm because they all liked her so much. She was a grandmother who was younger in spirit than her children. The men in the family loved her for her sense of humor, the children flocked around her because she understood them, and they all appreciated her for her wisdom and judgment.

As Jane walked along she could not shake the thought that something was going to happen for good or bad. What was the meaning of her aunt's brief letter, "It is always darkest before the dawn"?

13
A Bull in a China Shop

The opera singer began the new week in good spirits. By temperament she was a bright, optimistic person, and that was an added reason why the bouts of depression puzzled her. But she was fighting another cold and so she concluded that was the explanation for the undercurrent of discontent that swept over her more often than she cared to admit. She worked on the second act of *Norma* in the morning and recorded in her notebook, "Somehow I must search now for something to make me an exceptional singer. What is it I'm looking for besides experience? Perhaps it's heart and confidence. This is one opera I know from the skeleton on up, but now I must try to put flesh and blood into the personality of Norma...."

Instead of Jane's cold getting better, it got worse, and her performance at Cesena in the middle of October was a nightmare. She was forced to give up the second performance as the infection had settled in her throat and ears. It was her first experience where she could not go on, and she was certain it was the end of her career. She wrote in her diary, "Voice gradually going to pieces, and my heart with it."

She was forced to go away for a rest. At the time it seemed to be one of her lowest points, but in reality it

71

was a minor setback. In a few weeks when she returned to Milan her voice was stronger and richer than it had ever been.

On one of the nights following her illness, the telephone rang. It was the small stranger Jane had met on the church steps. She had tried to contact Jane several times when Jane was out of the city, and finally her persistence won out. Jane agreed to meet her the following Saturday evening.

When the night arrived, the singer was annoyed with herself for not saying, "No." She kept shaking her head while dressing and wondering at her weakness in giving the girl her telephone number. But then she had to laugh. She found herself again humming Wagner's destiny theme, and her annoyance disappeared and she went out into the night with a sense of expectancy.

As Jane walked up the stairs to the apartment where she had been told to go, for one brief moment she wanted to turn back and might have, but the "concierge" at the gate had already announced her.

A fine looking, intelligent lady opened the door and welcomed her. "My name is Georgia," she said with friendly reserve. A dark-haired, quietly vivacious person joined her, "and this is my friend, Maria Theresa."

She had deep brown eyes that looked inquiringly into Jane's eyes, with a suggestion of a smile, "I hope Anita didn't pressure you into coming!"

The opera singer liked her hostesses immediately. She said, "She is persistent, isn't she?"

They all laughed.

"Where is Anita? I hope I wasn't supposed to pick her up," Jane said.

"Oh no," said Georgia. "She'll be along shortly. She called to say she'd be late, it was something about her voice teacher. She has been after him for months to come to our class."

72

As they walked into the modest living room, Jane who had never heard about "a class" wondered what they were referring to, but at that moment Anita and a British girl, Vera, joined them, and Jane forgot about the class. In the midst of the greetings and introductions and Anita explaining why her voice professor was not able to come, Georgia called them into the kitchen for supper.

The opera singer particularly appreciated that her new friends treated her as a person rather than a figure in the theater. They were interested in music and her career and asked intelligent questions about it, but they didn't make over her or apologize because they had to entertain their guests in the kitchen. Jane enjoyed being treated as one of them and she delighted in the coziness of the kitchen meal. There were fresh flowers and candles on the table and just before the large platters of Italian ham, salami, cheese, salad and olives were passed, Maria Theresa asked Georgia to pray.

In commenting on this incident years later, Jane said, "It is curious the things you remember about people the first time you meet them. With me, it's usually the little things I remember. I'm not positive now who prayed that night—I think it was Georgia—nor can I recall what she said; but what I'll never forget is that she was talking to 'someone'! And then I wanted to cry when I realized it was the first table prayer I had heard since leaving Virginia. You see, when you are brought up in a family where your mother and father kneel by their bedside in prayer every night, even though you turn away from those values for a while, you are left with a strong memory that these things are not done for effect, but because of faith."

That evening as the conversation progressed around the kitchen table it did not take Jane long to deduce what sort of class was to follow. As they talked, Maria Theresa was figuring too. With frankness she announced there was to be a Bible study and that Miss Smith was not obligated to stay for it. Jane liked the sensitivity and openness of her new friend, and said, "In the first place, call me Jane, and in the second place, go right ahead with your study." She added expansively, "It might do me good! I have read through the Bible several times, but I find it terribly dull, and it has no relevance to the day in which we live."

As soon as the dishes were removed from the table, the study began. Jane recalls little of what was taught, but does remember that they had scarcely begun when she began asking impossible questions, ridiculing many of the things that were said and rudely interrupting at the least provocation. Nearly everything that was said that evening irritated her. "I was like a bull in a china shop," Jane later recalled, "and the more unpleasant and violent I became, the sweeter they were. They listened patiently to my crazy questions as if they deserved serious consideration! I couldn't get over how nice they were!"

When Maria Theresa called the opera singer in a few weeks to invite her to another buffet supper and Bible study, Jane said in amazement, "Do you mean you *really* want me to come again?"

Maria Theresa laughed in her gentle way, "Of course, we enjoyed having you and look forward to seeing you again."

14
A Lovely Surprise

Early in December Jane's Aunt Emma wrote at the end of a letter, "I hope Santa brings you a surprise engagement!"

And the same afternoon Jane was asked to sing an entire concert in Bergamo, because a famous Italian soprano had suddenly been taken ill. The concert was to take place the following evening.

There was confusion and excitement in Signora's apartment that evening getting the singer prepared for the unexpected performance. On her own Jane would not have had the confidence to step in at the last minute, but with Signora and Mary assuring her she could do it, she dared to believe so herself. Mary, who had fairly recently become Maestro's wife, was one of Jane's favorite friends. Both singers had graduated from Hollins College in Virginia, and through the years that Jane was in opera their paths often crossed. When Jane made her first trip to Italy as Maestro's newest pupil, Mary was already singing professionally, and in the early years of Jane's study she was a help and an encouragement. The singer's notebook in those days often said, "Mary said," or "Mary advised...."

Both Mary and Jane considered Signora Rolandi their Italian mother, and on this day the Italian mother and daughter, Mary, were pretending to be Maestro (who was in New York City), encouraging the other daughter. Mary said with feeling, "Salamona, you sing tomorrow as if it were the most important thing in the world!"

Then Signora shouted, waving her arms, "Don't be a little prima donna, be a *Big* prima donna!" and as she flung her arms back she knocked over a vase of flowers from the fireplace mantle. It fell dangerously near the beautiful dress which Jane was to wear for the concert. It sobered the trio and they stopped clowning as they settled down to the serious business of deciding what Jane should sing for the performance.

The next day Jane and Signora arrived in Bergamo (about a three hour drive from Milan) in time for the singer to have a rest at the hotel, followed by a brief rehearsal with a strange pianist and a tenor whom she knew, but with whom she had never sung. Then at the appointed hour, they were driven in a limousine to the Camozzi Palace, the private residence of the beloved Countess _____ of Bergamo, where a select audience had gathered for the special concert.

The group assembled in the music salon were there by invitation. Jane not only had a critical audience in front of her (Bergamo is an important musical city in Italy), but one looking forward to hearing an Italian star. How were they going to react to the American substitute, and a young one at that? Jane trembled inside, but the guests did not know that she had been waiting for just this sort of challenge. She had been singing exceptionally well in her lessons since her illness and was eager to sing in front of a discerning people. She intended to sing this night as if it were the most important thing in the world!

As Jane stepped forward to sing her first number, there was a power failure in the palace and all the lights went out. It was an awkward moment. Even a year before it might have unnerved her, but Maestro's insistence that a singer must remain poised *no matter what*, proved again how priceless his training was.

In what seemed like a long time, but actually was only a matter of minutes, several servants moved silently about the salon lighting candles, and four tall candelabra were brought to the platform. Two were placed on the grand piano, and one at either edge of the stage on stands which were quickly provided. When the soft candle glow reached the center of the stage, there stood the lovely, young singer, poised and serene, as if this was the way all her concerts began. A quiet murmur of approval moved across the large room. Even before her first note Jane had her audience with her. She sang with ease and had a liberated sense of really communicating with her listeners. Maestro, had he been there, would have wept with joy. It was the one thing he was still waiting for in Jane's singing, and it was the one thing he could not give her. It is something each singer must learn for himself, for herself—communication. Some never learn it, but the great artists all have it. It was said of Jenny Lind that the very power of her presence captivated the audience before she even opened her lips. That was what Jane experienced in Bergamo, and like the Swedish singer, she gave her best, "the very best of her best."

It is impossible to say what communication really is and it is more difficult to develop it; but it is certain that it can only happen after an artist has enough technique to forget technique. In the weeks preceding this concert, Jane had been working at freeing herself from her technique. Over and over in her notebook it is written, "Forget technique. Sing!"

"Get away from being a studied singer!"

"Sing freely!"

"Love to sing!"

And Jane had the thrill of doing that in Bergamo, and

when she majestically finished the aria, "Casta Diva," the delighted audience rose and shouted, "Brava!!"

After the concert there was a reception in the banquet hall with all the sumptuousness of the medieval age. By this time the electricity had come back on, and the crystal chandeliers with their brilliant light, and the evening dress of the guests were the only two indications that this was the twentieth century.

As many of the people wished to meet the American with the wonderful voice and warm personality, Jane got only a taste of the marvelous food which had been brought to her from the long table. The Countess finally rescued the singer from her many admirers and escorted her to a private table with two or three guests where they could enjoy the delicious repast and sparkling wines.

Jane noted in her diary the following day, "Concert, Bergamo, very successful." Then she added, "So much suffering is pulling something out of me."

15
A Stroll in the Park

The afternoon following the Bergamo success was warm and sunny. Maestro was still in New York, Mary was rehearsing for her Christmas performance, and Signora was in her kitchen. Jane came up behind Signora, untied her apron and said, "Go get yourself dressed up. We're going for a walk through the park, and later I'm treating us to ice cream at Motta's."

Signora did not need urging. She adored these rare promenades with her hard-working singers, and she was also very fond of ice cream. Jane had found it difficult to work after the exciting evening, and to have a warm, cheerful day in December in Milan was occasion enough to celebrate.

They walked through the zoo first and stopped to watch the elephant act. At the close of the piano routine, Jane put a bill out for the elephant. The big animal sniffed it and held it at the end of her trunk, and then instead of dropping it in the pocket of the trainer, she pretended to keep it herself. As they walked away laughing, Signora said, "That elephant is one of the best actresses in Milan!"

As they strolled through the park, Jane said, "It feels good to laugh. I surely haven't been the most cheerful person this year."

"You read too much and think too much, my dear," suggested Signora.

"Never!" Jane retorted. "Whoever reads too much? I wish I had more time than I do to read. I love learning, Signora. I want to learn. There's so much to learn."

"Yes, cara, but not when it makes you unhappy," Signora stuck to her point.

After walking for a while they found a bench near the lake. While they were sitting there, a poorly clad lady holding a baby walked up to them. Jane reached into her pocketbook and pressed some money into the dirty hand. After this had happened two or three times, Signora suggested they move.

"Yes," said Jane, "let's have our ice cream."

When they arrived at the tearoom, they decided it was warm enough to sit outside.

"Oh," said Jane, throwing back her arms, "isn't it good to breathe fresh air again!"

It wasn't all that fresh. Milan is one of the most industrial centers in Italy, but to Jane it was wonderful to be sitting on the edge of the park at least looking at trees and grass.

While they were waiting for a waiter to discover them, a strolling violin player came and serenaded them, and Jane tipped him generously. When Signora frowned at the generosity of the tip, Jane replied, "I believe in supporting musicians."

Soon the waiter came, and the opera singer (with Maestro far away in America) ordered the specialty of the house for both of them, homemade vanilla ice cream with fresh fruit and a mountain of whipped cream. While they were waiting for the treat, a small boy played "Yankee Doodle" on a harmonica. Jane dipped again into her pocketbook. "You Americans!" was all Signora said with a mixture of scorn and affection.

After the ice cream they lingered over coffee talking

and laughing as two people without a care in the world. The beautiful day seemingly had drawn out every down-and-out musician and beggar in Northern Italy. With the coffee they were entertained by an accordion player with a dancing monkey. The opera singer clapped loudly at the end of the act, and when the monkey tipped his hat and held up his cup, a fistful of coins clinked in. He tipped his hat again, loudly shaking the tin cup and began dancing again for the bountiful singer.

"I hate to think of leaving," Signora said, "but I do have a few things left undone in my kitchen."

"Of course," said Jane, "we've been here a long time."

She then reached once more into the alligator pocketbook to pay for their refreshments. She frowned as she tried to find something that didn't seem to be there, and with one of her impulsive gestures, Jane dumped the entire contents of her bag out on the table.

"Signora!" she exclaimed, as she frantically went through the contents on the table, "I don't have a cent left! Not even a hundred lira!" In a lower voice she said, "Do you mind letting me have some money, and I'll pay you back the minute we get home?" She laughed, "Isn't this ridiculous!"

In the meantime Signora was shuffling through her large, leather pocketbook, and she said with a startled expression on her face, "Jane, I don't think I have my billfold with me!" She groped some more, and whispered, "No, it simply isn't here! What'll we do?"

Jane sighed, "Well, I'm glad I haven't called the waiter. I almost did, but then he slipped by."

It must be remembered that in Europe you can sit all day and all night at a cafe table and your waiter won't come near you until you summon him, and then even when summoned, some waiters are slow in coming. The system is the reverse of the American way which likes to keep people moving, and so the two desperate ones had time to work out a solution. Jane was tempted to do the straightforward thing and simply tell the waiter their problem and come back and pay tomorrow, but she didn't suggest it. It was too easy. An Italian much prefers doing something the hard way to "save face." Signora, in the meantime, had worked out a solution. She whispered to Jane, "I've my checkbook with me, so you stay here at the table, and I'll go over to the bakery on the edge of the park. I know the lady who runs it, and she'll cash a check for me."

By the time Signora came back with money to pay their bill the sun was about to set, and by walking briskly they arrived home before dark. Signora spent the evening telling Mary about their afternoon. Particularly she enjoyed demonstrating how Jane dipped into her pocketbook passing out money to the left and to the right. Jane who was trying to write a letter at the desk in the living room finally gave up and joined in on the laughter.

16
The Final Fling

Things moved swiftly once Jane started going to the Bible study. She still was not sure what her new friends were trying to say, but she liked the way they said it. She kept returning for further stimulating talk in the kitchen. She had learned also that Georgia and Maria Theresa were missionaries, but by this time she liked them so much, she forgave them for their poor taste in having chosen such a profession.

Towards the end of 1955 the group was meeting twice a month at the request of the singer who was trying to get in as much instruction as possible before Maestro returned from America. She wasn't sure what he would say or do about her new interest, but he certainly could not say it had harmed her voice. In her heart she knew that she was singing better than the last time he had heard her.

At one of the meetings there was a visitor from Switzerland, a professor who was also a writer. Like Maria Theresa, he spoke with quiet authority. He told the group squeezed into the living room of the small apartment, about the unusual circumstances in his life which caused him to leave his law office and become a teacher of the Bible. It was an interesting story and very dramatic, which appealed to the singer. Towards the end of his talk he said that the Bible had meant nothing to him until he had had a personal encounter with the Lord Jesus Christ.

Later in the evening when Jane was saying goodbye to Maria Theresa, she asked, "What did he mean about a personal encounter?" And before she finished that question, she asked another, "How do you know someone who has been dead nearly two thousand years? The professor seemed like such an intelligent man until he said that."

"It could happen to you too, Jane," said the missionary with gentleness.

The tall opera singer looked down at her friend and exclaimed more loudly than she meant, "Happen to me!! How...."

"It is quite simple," was the soft answer from the one with the lively brown eyes. "Ask the Lord to come into your life."

As several other people were preparing to leave and thanking Maria Theresa for the evening, they did not get to finish their conversation.

With Maestro coming back in a few days, Jane had little time for reflection, and so the professor's talk, her questions and Maria Theresa's answer had to be filed in a back compartment of her mind. With the warrior-teacher to be soon in their midst. Signora Rolandi, Mary and Jane decided to have a final fling.

They invited several other musicians to the apartment for a special dinner. The two singers did the shopping and selected all the foods and beverages they liked the best, and Signora did the rest. One of the tenors arrived carrying a huge azalea plant wrapped in silver paper and with an enormous red bow. It was a festive, hilarious evening and the friends ate, talked, laughed and toasted Maestro until early in the morning. Signora, after she finished serving the meal, sat down at the table and entered into the fun, chanting, "When the cat's away, the mice will play!"

The next morning they slept late, at least the singers did. Around eleven, Signora brought them coffee, and told them that they were all invited to dinner that evening at a friend's home. She announced, "I accepted for all of us."

Before Jane and Mary could protest, she said firmly, "Let me finish. We have eaten everything in the house, and it is either go out tonight or have soup and water."

As they still did not seem convinced, she added, "It is your last chance to step out for a long time!"

Even though Maestro was now Mary's husband, he was foremost her voice teacher and she was subjected to the same rigorous discipline as the other students. Even from across the ocean he tried to control his pupils, but with not quite the same success as when he was right with them. The reason he was in New York was to earn more money, but he telephoned Milan frequently. It was difficult for them to understand how he was getting ahead financially with the telephone bills he had to pay, but they complained not a word while enjoying their freedom.

Late in the afternoon they started to dress for their evening engagement. Signora was the first to be ready.

"Our problem now," she said, "is what to take our hostess. Some candy or...." (It is unheard of in Italy to accept an invitation with friends and not take a gift.)

"I've got it," said Mary. "We'll take the azalea."

"No, we couldn't possibly do that," exclaimed Signora. "It was a present to us, and don't forget, we go right past Rossolini's apartment."

"We're going to have to take it," Mary insisted. "I don't have any money. Jane, JANE," she shouted. "How much money do you have?"

"Money," exploded Jane from the bedroom. "None, of course, I spent my last lira yesterday on our party.

"Then it's settled," Mary said, "We take the plant."

And so the three fashionably attired ladies with their evening bags glittering with jewels and nothing in them, stepped out into the evening with Signora walking in the middle carrying the large azalea plant wrapped in silver paper with the red bow around it.

As they approached the building where the tenor lived, who had given them the plant, Signora whispered nervously, "What will we say if he looks out the window?"

"We'll tell him, 'Good evening!' " suggested Mary.

"And," Jane added, "if he should notice the plant, we can say, 'We are taking it for a walk.' "

Signora burst into a peal of laughter and in her attempt to muffle it almost dropped the azalea.

"Quiet!" ordered Mary. Jane was laughing too, causing several eyes to turn and look at them. Mary had the most sang-froid of the trio, and at last marshalled the other two safely past Rossolini's apartment building. By the time they reached their destination they were composed and playing again the role of the "grandes dames." Very properly and with a correct amount of cordial reserve Signora presented the plant to their hostess....

That night, after another sumptuous dinner, the two mice and the fairy godmother tiptoed home, put away the party gowns, and with a few deep sighs, started to prepare themselves for the stormy sessions ahead.

17
A Small Hinge

Jane did not attend many Bible studies after Maestro came back from America. It wasn't that he wouldn't let her go, but there simply was not time. Soon after his return she signed a contract to sing the lead role in the opera, *Norma*, in a theater near Milan.

She had been studying the part for years, but now, with the performance ahead, the work was intensified. Above all in opera is the singing, of course, but the interpreting of the roles and the acting also have to be worked out. Because singing makes such physical demands on the performer, it imposes limitations on movement and gestures and makes operatic acting very difficult. Jane's goal was to make Norma convincing, and so in the winter months of 1956 she spent hours simply reading and thinking about the subject she was to portray. It was not enough for her to sing Norma, look like Norma and act like Norma. She wanted to be Norma on the stage. This took time and effort.

The last Bible class she attended before losing herself in *Norma* was a study from Philippians about "rejoicing in the Lord." You would have thought it would appeal to Jane who from childhood had exhibited an unusually happy, exuberant spirit, but the study disturbed her. It made her wonder about the reality of her happiness and upon what it was actually based. But she did not bother about it after she signed the new contract. From then on she was more aware of Norma's feelings than her own.

One other thing happened that night at the class which should be mentioned, one of the small hinges in life upon which a mighty door swings open. It was only an invitation from an American family living in the Swiss Alps. As Georgia said, "Any of you who want to get away from Milan for a few days are invited. I think it takes about five hours by train."

"I'd love to go," Anita said, and turning to Jane she said, "Let's go together, Jane. You're always talking about how much you love the country."

"I couldn't possibly," she answered impatiently. "I'm far too busy, and anyway, you know Maestro, he'd be wild if I went off even for a weekend!"

Even though Jane again had mixed emotions about the hours he made her keep and the exhausting lessons they had, she was at the same time glad to be working with him again. She noted in her diary: "The only person in the world who understands my voice!"

It was true, Maestro did understand her voice, and he became more ambitious than ever for her when he saw and heard the progress she had made in the past year. What he did not understand was the complexity of her mind and seeking spirit. Here the two friends, the teacher and his pupil, were strangers. Opera for Maestro was not only a way of life or something to do in life, it was life. It was a mystery to him why Jane reached for something more.

The grinding work, the strict hours went on for a couple of months. Then in April, when spring should have moved over northern Italy caressing, awakening and warming the shivering life huddled under the chilly blanket of fog, the weather became colder and damper. Impulsively Jane called her missionary friends. "Georgia, it's Jane," she said. "You mentioned that family in Switzerland some time ago. I've got to get out of Milan for a few days. The weather is driving me out of my mind. I'm so chilled, and it's a perfect time for me to sneak away. Maestro had to go out of town!" Jane gave one of her big laughs. "Do you mind giving me their name and address again? I'm going to call Anita first and see if she still wants to go, then I'll send—what's their name? Oh, yes, the Schaeffers, a telegram."

They talked a bit longer, and immediately after Jane put down the phone she picked it up again and called Anita who was also delighted at the prospect of getting away from dreary Milan. So the telegram was sent announcing their arrival.

The opera singer had a vague suspicion the Schaeffers were also missionaries. Who else freely would open their homes to people they've never met? But her experience with Georgia and Maria Theresa had made her considerably less bothered with missionaries in general. Her main object for the weekend was to escape the damp and chill of Milan.

18
A Bombshell Question

Switzerland was as dreary and damp as Italy that Easter weekend, and much colder. As Anita and Jane hurried up the path to Chalet les Melezes they saw a man working in the garden. He quickly put down the shovel with which he was trying to dig in the frozen ground, and walked towards them.

"I'm Mr. Schaeffer," he said. "I'm happy you are able to spend Easter with us." He shrugged his shoulders, "Wish we could have provided better weather for you! I know it is hard to believe," he pointed into the fog, "but starting up at Villars, the ski resort above us," he made a large arc with his hand, "all across in front of us and down to the Rhone Valley, are mountains." He smiled, "It's a marvelous view on a clear day!"

At that moment a young girl and a small boy burst out the side door and ran down the steps to welcome the two guests. Frankie made a dive for the two overnight bags before his sister could pick them up.

"Come on in," he said cordially. "We made a big fire in the fireplace, I mean, Susan made the fire, I carried in the wood. We always make a fire when Americans come."

His father laughed, "Frankie makes it sound as if we're not Americans. It's just that we are not American

90

in some of our habits. Please do go inside, Anita and Jane. Mrs. Schaeffer will be down in a moment with some hot tea."

The Schaeffers' large chalet with two balconies across the front was on the edge of a small, rural village. As they stepped into the hallway, Jane observed that it was colder than outside, but she cheered up when she saw the large fireplace at the far end of the tastefully furnished, panelled living room. The sound of the crackling, popping wood burning in the fireplace was music to her ears.

Susan and Frankie kept them entertained until their mother brought the tea. She greeted the two strangers with the same sincere friendliness her husband and children had. Jane could not help but think "what a contrast this family is to so many people I know in the theater with their artificiality. There is something genuine about these people, they are not putting on charm the way we do in opera."

Mrs. Schaeffer, at the same time Jane was puzzling about her and her family, was wondering about Jane. The Schaeffers had assumed Anita and Jane were gospel singers, members of some "team" touring churches in Europe, and Mrs. Schaeffer was thinking as she looked at the fashionably dressed person sitting in front of her with a large diamond on her finger, pearl earrings which matched the antique pin (with pearls and diamonds) which she was wearing and the beautiful fur coat thrown casually back over the chair—what a gospel singer!

When Susan helped her mother carry the tea things up to the kitchen, she said excitedly, "Oh, Mother, they're not gospel singers, they're opera singers! At least, Jane is, and Anita is studying to be one too, she said. Isn't it thrilling!!!"

"Shhhhh! They might hear you." Mrs. Schaeffer whispered to her daughter."

She was as excited as Susan, but better able to contain it, all except the large, dancing brown eyes.

"We won't do the dishes now," the mother said, "We'll...."

Debby and Pris came in from doing errands. And Susan rushed over to her sisters. "The guests from Milan are here and they're OPERA singers!"

Debby, who was the youngest, clapped her hands together and squealed, "How marvelous! I've always wanted to meet a real live opera singer!"

"Shhh, be quiet," the older sister declared. "You two have about as much sophistication as Monsieur Ruchet's goats. So they are opera singers. Poff, they're just people like...."

Pris didn't get to finish her remark. The mother of the three lively girls took command, "Debby, you can set the table, and Susan, you arrange the centerpiece and candles. I've started to clean the salad but you can finish it, Priscilla, and at the same time you all can be praying. I'm going down now to have a talk with our guests."

When Mrs. Schaeffer returned to the living room on the ground floor, Jane was standing in front of the fire in a very dramatic pose listening to Frankie who was attempting to look equally as theatrical with one hand on his chest and the other making important gestures as he was telling about some of the more colorful people who had visited them in their chalet. Anita was sitting on the stone bench to the side of the fireplace also listening to Frankie.

Very soon after his mother entered the room Frankie was sent out to help his father, and the three new friends sat down to get acquainted with one another. Jane noticed two things about her hostess which captured her attention, besides the fact that she was an attractive, dynamic person. Even as she spoke, and she spoke in a vivid and animated way, there was still a quality of listening about her, as if she were listening beyond the person sitting next to her. Jane remarked again how warm and genuinely concerned she was. She thought to herself, "How Virginian, how southern she is!"

Several hours later Jane was again seated by the fireplace in the living room, this time talking with Mr. Schaeffer. It surprised and interested the opera singer how much he knew about music and art, her two great interests, and she quickly discovered that he was an avid reader like herself. She kept thinking "I know they are missionaries, but they don't act like it."

The dinner, which had been not only delicious, but festive, also became riotous. Debby and Susan, particularly, kept asking Jane to tell about life in the opera world, and the singer obligingly, with gestures and much laughter herself, told some of the humorous things that had happened to her on the stage.

Relaxed and enjoying herself in the cheerful atmosphere of the mountain chalet, Jane was taken off guard when in the course of their conversation about the religious significance of Wagner's music, Mr. Schaeffer asked casually, "Jane, are you a Christian?"

Even though he asked the question in the way in which one might ask, "Are you an American?" or "Are you an artist?" it was a bombshell question to the opera singer. It stirred up something far below the surface. She answered coldly, "I think I am."

The question annoyed her. She thought, "I'm certainly as Christian as you are, Mr. Missionary." The two were unable to explore the question further, as at that moment the others came down from the kitchen after doing the dishes. Before the children had to go to bed, they had a few more questions for Jane about opera. She talked with them for a while, and then Mrs. Schaeffer left with them to see that they went to bed. Anita had a few questions for Mr. Schaeffer. They were soon involved in a discussion about the relevancy of the Bible in the twentieth century. Jane, who had been told to make herself at home, after a polite interval, excused herself and also retired.

The night that followed was far from comfortable. Her mind turned over many questions, "Why did I bother to come here? What am I looking for? Why can't I learn to be content in my own world of opera? No one asks questions there about what you believe. Why do I insist upon thinking there is more in life? That there should be more than what I see with my eyes?" The hot water bottle Mrs. Schaeffer brought to her did not quite remove the mountain chill in the airy, four-bed room. She was cold, but what kept her awake more than the chill in her bones were the questions in her mind, particularly Mr. Schaeffer's question. Early in the morning as she noisily turned over in one of the top bunks, causing Anita to sit up in alarm, she said out loud, "I certainly am a Christian," and went to sleep.

19
Enthusiastic about Religion

The fog and grey of Sunday morning finally came. After breakfast Anita and Jane were invited to attend the family church service conducted by Mr. Schaeffer in the living room. By this time Jane had learned that her host was a Presbyterian minister. Exactly what he and his family were doing in this Swiss chalet on the edge of a small mountain village was not clear to her. Her feelings toward them were similar to her feelings toward Georgia and Maria Theresa: whatever they were doing, she liked the way they were doing it. Her irritation with Mr. Schaeffer was gone. Jane was not one to hold grudges or stay mad about something said to her which she did not like. Before the service began Mrs. Schaeffer asked Jane if she would play the piano for the hymns.

"One of the girls usually plays, but as Debby said (and Mrs. Schaeffer mimicked her daughter in such an amusing way, it completely restored Jane's good humor), 'With a *real* live opera star in our home, I couldn't *possibly* play this morning!' "

Jane enjoyed playing and singing the hymns with the others. As Susan whispered loudly to Frankie, "We almost sound like a whole churchful singing." It felt good to the singer to be sitting in this makeshift chapel worshipping with these new friends. Thoughtfully someone had built another big fire in the fireplace and saw to it that the two guests were seated near it.

After church even Jane stepped into the kitchen and made a pretense of helping in the midst of the preparation of the special Easter dinner. Mrs. Schaeffer had an excellent helper, Dorothy. Dot was an American college student who had visited them for a weekend and had stayed on to assist with the work.

Standing in one corner of the tiny kitchen, Jane could scarcely believe that on a normal weekend they often served twenty or thirty people from the same little kitchen. Debby and Susan were coloring eggs. Frankie was walking excitedly back and forth, first in front of Jane, then Anita, telling them how many eggs he had found in last year's Easter egg hunt, and the year before, and before that, and....

He trailed Jane into the dining room where she was helping Dot set the table. They were having a deep conversation about the Holy Spirit. Frankie entered right in. He asked Jane if she knew Hudson Taylor (he had seen Jane leaf through his biography which was lying on the buffet), "You ought to read about him. Boy, he really knew how to pray!"

By this time Dot was explaining that in order for prayer to reach God a person needs the power of the Holy Spirit in his life. Jane was thinking, as she was trying to follow the different stimulating conversations (there was another one going on in the kitchen), "I've never heard so many people in one house talk so knowingly and enthusiastically about religion in all my life. It wouldn't surprise me if Susan, even Debby, teach Sunday School."

Finally the dinner was ready. When Mr. Schaeffer said, "Debby, will you pray for us," the young girl prayed as if the Lord was right there in the chalet and personally interested in each one sitting around the table. Jane nodded within herself, "If she doesn't teach Sunday School, she surely could."

It was a lovely meal. Mrs. Schaeffer had arranged a new centerpiece (it made Jane think of her mother's beautiful dinner parties in Virginia), and in front of each place was a small Easter basket full of candy. Again Jane was stirred by the thoughtfulness, artistic sensitivity and warmth of this family. The children tried to get her to talk about opera again, but she had competition. Nearly all the Schaeffers enjoy talking, and Jane marveled at the way they wove in something about God, the Bible or Christianity with art, music, history, politics or whatever happened to be mentioned, and in a realistic and interesting way. They sat at the table a long time, but it seemed like only a few minutes to Jane.

There was a moment of silence at the end of the meal, after the devotional reading and prayer, and Jane, whose sensitive ears miss little, opened her eyes and looked at the antique clock which had just made an odd clicking sound. It was still raining outside, and the streaking rain on the window panes reflected into the glass on the clock, making it look like tears running down its face. In that fleeting, hushed moment Jane knew she could not leave this village without discovering the secret of the aliveness and joy of this family which seemed to spring up from inside them.

After the Easter hunt, which Frankie made everyone participate in, Mrs. Schaeffer and Jane took a walk through the village. It had stopped raining, but it was still grey and foggy. As they walked down the steep, narrow road past chalets which were several hundred years old and art objects in themselves with the carved, wooden balconies, each with a different design, and thick, weathered walls, Jane kept shaking her head and repeating, "Beautiful, beautiful." They stopped to admire a large, antique kettle hanging from a chain

97

fastened under the edge of the roof. Mrs. Schaeffer said, "You should see it in the summer with bright, red geraniums in it! The flowers in this small village are a story in themselves. All the window boxes have flowers, and the Swiss ladies put flowers in shoes, all kinds of pots, boxes and old wagons, besides in regular gardens."

As Jane's eyes swept beyond the village, she had another treat. The gently sloping fields in front of the chalets were filled with wild flowers. "How I wish the sun would come out," said Mrs. Schaeffer. "It brings out the color more vividly, not to mention the mountains!"

They continued down the road, and Jane noticed how neatly the wood was stacked under the wide, overhanging eaves. "You should see the wonderful vegetables we grow here too," Mrs. Schaeffer said, and as they were passing one of the many village manure piles, she added with a laugh, "There's the secret to the green in Switzerland!"

As they started to move away from the strong-scented heap, the opera star stopped, took a deep breath, spread wide her arms as if she were about to sing an aria, and exclaimed, "I love the smell of manure!"

After Mrs. Schaeffer could catch her breath from laughing (she had never heard a remark quite like that), she took another look at her weekend guest and said, "Forgive me for laughing, Jane, I really believe you mean it. Many of our city visitors look around politely, marvel at the mountains, of course, but find nothing beautiful in our village. But you really like it."

The opera singer was laughing too. After she said it she too realized how funny it sounded.

"It's true, though, I do love the smell of a farm," she said enthusiastically. "I love the country. I love gardens. I love cows. I love chickens. It all reminds me of Virginia and the horses I used to ride across the fields." She added, rather fiercely (the mood of the singer could change as quickly as a summer storm), "There are times I hate my career, always in big, dirty cities, and so much make-believe and unending pretending...." Quickly she said, "Don't misunderstand. I love being an opera singer. I love singing. I'd never give it up. It's my life, but...." Wistfully she added, "You don't know what it means to me to be here this weekend."

Jane found it easy to talk to Mrs. Schaeffer. There was a comfortable bond between them as they walked back through the village, past the fountain by the schoolhouse, around the white church with the large plane tree in front of it, and on up the steep path. It was getting near the time of the high tea, and Mrs. Schaeffer wanted to make some orange rolls and assorted sandwiches for her guests from Italy.

Jane was glad to return to the fireplace. By this time the singer felt as if she had known the Schaeffer family a long time, and when towards the end of the tea—and it was a lovely tea—the conversation again smoothly turned to spiritual matters, Jane found herself hungry to hear every word.

Mr. Schaeffer was speaking about what it meant to be a Christian in the real sense of the word, and not what the twentieth-century man means when he says he is a Christian. Jane had bristled the night before when Mr. Schaeffer had asked her if she was a Christian, because she thought he was asking her about her conduct or way of life. She listened carefully as he explained that a Christian is a person who believes in God, who acts on the knowledge which is given to him in the Bible, and the Bible says that salvation is obtained by faith in Christ plus nothing. A person is not saved on the basis of the strength of his faith, but on the object of his faith.

"Yes, but what about the morality of a person and the

99

good things he does in his life, surely they are important to a Christian, aren't they?" Jane asked.

"Of course," said Mr. Schaeffer. "I am stressing the other side of the coin which is often ignored today, that our eternal destiny rests upon what God has done for man, and not what man has done, is doing and will do for God. Our churches are filled with people today who are trusting their 'good' works, their 'good' conduct to save them. How can I know I'm a Christian? By believing God. Believing what He says will save me."

Towards the end of the evening when the fire in the fireplace was reduced to a few glowing coals, Mr. Schaeffer picked up his worn Bible and read from the book of John, "There was a man of the Pharisees named Nicodemus, a ruler of the Jews. The same came to Jesus by night and said unto him, Rabbi, we know that thou art a teacher come from God, for no man can do these miracles that thou doest, except God be with him." Jane listened carefully while he read, straining to see if it had meaning for her. Mr. Schaeffer went on, "Jesus answered and said unto him, verily, verily, I say unto thee, except a man be born again, he cannot see the kingdom of God...." He read on and finished on John 3:16, "For God so loved the world that he gave his only begotten Son, that whosoever believeth in him should not perish but have everlasting life."

The opera singer went to bed that night with the words of Jesus ringing in her ears.

Singer Jane Stuart Smith by the hearth in her Alpine chalet

Debut in Venice

Photo: Giacomelli

Jane Stuart Smith in Milan

Dr. Francis Schaeffer and family

Betty Carlson in front of the Swiss Alps

Flentrop Organ in L'Abri Chapel

Jane Stuart Smith

Chalet at L'Abri

Author Betty Carlson

20
A Shaft of Light

Monday came, the day Jane and Anita had planned to leave on the five o'clock bus to catch the Paris-Milan train in Aigle down in the Rhone Valley. In the afternoon, Mr. Schaeffer invited Jane to take a walk with him. As they started up the steep steps at the back of the chalet, the conversation flowed on from the night before.

By now Jane had grasped that for Mr. Schaeffer, the Bible was the Word of God. In this short weekend she had heard him say more than once that there is no point in paying any attention to the Bible or to Christianity unless you take them seriously. A loose view of Scripture results in a loose view of God, whereas a man who holds to Scripture is not only in the right stream doctrinally, but historically too. It was electrifying to Jane to hear a twentieth-century man, and a theologian at that, who spoke with conviction about God Who is personal and deals with men personally, not mechanically as machines. She found it refreshing to hear about the Living God Who hears what His people have to say to Him. This was news to Jane. Good news. The books she had read, the clergymen she had heard all talked about the great gulf between God and man.

As they walked on, Mr. Schaeffer began to explain to the singer what a wonderful unity exists between the Old and New Testaments. Jane was stunned to learn that there were scholarly persons in our advanced civilization who still took the Old Testament seriously, and even more, linked it closely with the New Testament. Jane, the artist and musician, as well as knowledgeable in all the arts including literature and history, had a great respect for the concept of "relationship." What had made the Bible of such small importance to her was the seeming lack of relatedness. No one before Mr. Schaeffer had ever caused her to see that the Old Testament was related to the New, and that each of the books in the Bible had a definite connecting link, and the entire miraculous Book was related to her, had something to say to her as she lived and walked, breathed and sang in the last half of the twentieth century. As they arrived at a high point above the village, Mr. Schaeffer looked at his watch. "Oh, I'm terribly sorry," he said, "we must turn back here or you'll miss your bus."

"You were saying...."

Jane couldn't have cared less about the bus, or twenty buses, or two thousand times two million buses. There was a mounting excitement within her as she was getting closer to what she had been seeking so long; it was as if she needed only a few pieces and the jigsaw puzzle would be completed.

Mr. Schaeffer began speaking about Abraham. Abraham—who had been such an enigma to Jane most of her life. And suddenly her eyes were opened to the wonder of how God had provided a sacrifice to take Isaac's place at the last moment, and then, how two thousand years later, God allowed the Lord Jesus Christ to be offered up for the sins of each person who would believe in Him.

Jane's orderly mind began to piece together the

awesome fact that the God of the Bible is Who He says He is, the God of all history, and He has revealed Himself in Scripture for all ages. She did not have to say it out loud, but suddenly, and yet not so suddenly, she believed. She believed God, and she believed in His only Son, the Lord Jesus Christ.

As her heart and mind were attempting to take it all in, simultaneously came the realization that by the Spirit of God, the Living God, to Whom she had cried out from the airplane high above the Nile River almost one year ago, she had been brought to this place, at this moment, to have her eyes opened to truth, God's truth.

The weight of sin which had pressed down for so long upon the opera singer, but had never been defined as sin, fell from her shoulders like Christian in *Pilgrim's Progress*, when his load of sin fell and disappeared in the hole at the foot of the cross, and a great flood of joy came into her heart.

God Who is personal and deals individually with His people proved to the opera star that day that the theater is colorless compared to His pageants. While the singer and missionary were speaking, the fog, which had been hanging heavily upon the mountains, village and fields of flowers, suddenly broke apart and a magnificent shaft of light poured down upon the earth. For the first time, Jane saw the majestic mountains in front of them and all around them, and the flowers at their feet were brighter, just as Mrs. Schaeffer said they would be.

"Amazing," was all Jane could say.

It was so spectacular Jane could not find the words to tell the Schaeffers what had happened to her. There was no doubt in her mind that she had stepped from darkness into light, but it was such a vital moment she felt the need to return to Milan to test the reality of her conversion.

The opera singer spent the rest of her visit in the

chalet joking and laughing with the children, helping in the kitchen and talking with Mrs. Schaeffer. When the two singers left on the bus the following day, the Schaeffer family had no idea that Jane had made a significant decision on that hill above the village.

She spent the first day of her return to Milan shut up in her bedroom, carefully going through the Bible studies which Mr. Schaeffer had given her. Then, after she prayed, she wrote two letters to her friends in the Alps. The first was a thank you note intimating that something special had happened to her.

"Please accept this small gift," she wrote, "to help in some way with the glorious work you are doing for God and mankind. I can only wish that you will continue to influence other people's lives as you have mine.... Again may I thank you with all my heart for my visit to L'Abri. Forgive me if this letter has taken a long time to finish. I wanted to be sure the afterglow would not fade. The light grows brighter each day...."

The entire family could scarcely wait for the next letter, and when it came it brought tears of joy and enthusiastic praise to God for honoring their prayers and conversations with the opera singer that Easter weekend.

She wrote, "When Georgia spoke of you in our Bible class and mentioned the possibility of a visit, I was not in the least interested, and later said quite flatly that I'd never find time for such a thing. Now I am perfectly certain that I was led to L'Abri by a power quite outside myself. I now believe it was the Holy Spirit leading me forward in God's plan for my life. And that it was right for me to miss the bus and have the few hours necessary to accept Jesus Christ as my Saviour.

"Indeed, I feel that the power of Christ's spirit has opened my blinded eyes to the true light. You, dear Dr. and Mrs. Schaeffer, have quietly and simply shown me the pathway I have been searching for so long...."

And the opera singer, who until *that* weekend, had found the Bible dull and of no consequence for her life, asked her friends if they would mind writing the following verses from Luke 18:35-43 in their guestbook:

And it came to pass, that as he was come nigh unto Jericho, a certain blind man sat by the wayside begging: And hearing the multitude pass by, he asked what it meant. And they told him that Jesus of Nazareth passeth by.

And he cried saying, Jesus, thou son of David, have mercy on me. And they which went before rebuked him, that he should hold his peace: But he cried so much the more, Thou son of David, have mercy on me.

And Jesus stood and commanded him to be brought unto him: and when he was come near, he asked him,

Saying, What wilt thou that I shall do unto thee? And he said, Lord, that I may receive my sight.

And Jesus said unto him, Receive thy sight: Thy faith hath saved thee.

And immediately he received his sight, and followed him, glorifying God. And all the people, when they saw it, gave praise unto God.

21
On the Way

Three "immediatelys" followed Jane's Easter weekend in the Swiss Alps. Immediately she started reading the Bible. She reasoned that if the Scriptures truly are God's verbalized revelation to man, she owed it not only to herself, but to God to get some idea as speedily as she could what He has spoken. She began pursuing the Word of God with the same intensity as an opera score. She was not satisfied merely to read the words, nor settle for a pocket-sized devotional book. Not Jane. In those first few weeks after her conversion it would be difficult to estimate how many letters passed between Jane and the Schaeffers, or how many questions she asked; but soon she was outfitted with maps, commentaries, Bible dictionaries, various translations and a set of new notebooks in which to write down the things she wished to remember.

The second "immediately." Immediately she started speaking to others about what had happened to her in Switzerland. One of the first phone calls was to Maria Theresa and Georgia to tell them the great news, and in the same breath (when excited, Jane rarely uses punctuation in speaking), she asked if the monthly Bible class, which for her benefit was now meeting twice a month, could be held once a week. And within days she had spoken to several opera friends about the peace and joy she now had and of her amazement to learn that God is personally interested in people.

And third. Immediately Jane discovered that she was in the arena of the supernatural world, and that the chief adversary, Satan, was not the grinning, red-cloaked clown of masquerade balls, but a deadly enemy.

On April 5th, 1956, she recorded that she had had a lesson with one of the conductors in Milan and that they had worked on Acts I and II of *Norma*, and then instead of the usual comments on how she sang and what the conductor had said, she wrote, "A trip to visit an American missionary family in Switzerland, Dr. Francis Schaeffer. A spiritual revelation. Now with God and Christ on my side and the Holy Spirit with me always, I have found the way ... am an entirely different person and singer. I am no longer afraid and walking in the dark. I can do it now, because I'm no longer alone."

Maestro came back to Milan in the middle of April, and as the *Norma* production was only a couple of weeks away, Jane felt it wiser *not* to go into detail, or say *anything*, about her weekend in the Alps. He had heard from several sources that his "Bella Salamona" had met some "religious fanatics" and was talking strangely, but he decided to ignore whatever had happened until *after* the important engagement. The main thing now was to put the finishing touches on *Norma*.

Jane was thinking, "If I can prove to Maestro that my singing is better than ever because of my new faith in God, then he will be for it." And Maestro had it figured out, "If she sings *Norma* as I think she is going to, from now on, she'll be so in demand on the stage there won't be a waking moment for religious nonsense. It will be squeezed out."

They worked hard the next two weeks, and when the evening of the general rehearsal came Jane was amazed what a calming effect prayer had upon her. Few people, even opera-lovers, have any idea of the tension, confusion and accumulated emotional furor which surges about backstage. Some of the rehearsals are flashbacks to Dante's *Inferno*. The coarseness of the language sometimes rises about the singing and it is not without provocation. Sometimes singers are obliged to sing together with little or no rehearsal. On occasion the conductor who rules an Italian performance with an iron hand will have it in for a certain singer and drive him to a point of near insanity. And there are the usual jealousies, the mean, petty acts desperate people are capable of when fighting to stay on top. But the audience rarely sees any of this.

Then it was May 2 and the night of the *Norma* performance. It was an exciting evening. After the last curtain call the audience, and even the orchestra members, rose to their feet and shouted "Brava! Bravissima!" And the theater echoed with expressions of approval for the poised, leading lady.

But the words that sounded the sweetest to the star of the performance came from Maestro, "First rate, cara! You and I are going places, Salamona. Anyone who sang Norma the way you did tonight can sing anything, anywhere!"

Jane had never seen Maestro happier. He was as busy as she shaking hands, embracing admirers who had pushed into the star's dressing room. He continued ecstatically, "You go on singing like you did tonight, cara, and the impresarios from around the world will be knocking on your door!"

It was no surprise to Maestro the following day when the impresario from the Teatro Massimo Bellini in Catania, one of the leading opera houses in Europe, came with a contract for the American prima donna to open the fall season in *Die Walküre*, in the role she longed most of all to sing, Brunnhilde.

"What did I tell you?" smiled Maestro, after the singer had signed the contract with a flair becoming to a relative of the colorful General J. E. B. Stuart of Virginia. At the same time, tears came into his eyes.

"You know how I love my pupils, Salamona," he said fiercely, "I care for them all, but they are not all thoroughbreds." Gently he added, "My deepest dreams and fondest hopes are lodged in you and Mary. Don't...."

He walked over and pretended to be engrossed in something he saw out of the window while he composed himself. When he turned back, he gripped Jane by her hands and looked deeply into her eyes. Going directly to the point he said, "Don't do anything foolish, cara. Religion is fine, good, a wonderful thing, and I am happy you have found something to fill up that hole in the middle." He smiled gently, and said firmly, "But don't ever let it compete with opera! Opera is your life. Some people are painters, doctors, a few missionaries, others teachers," proudly he exclaimed, "and you, my dear, are an opera singer—a real prima donna! Don't forget it, and don't let anything come before it, NOT—EVEN—*GOD*.'

Jane had it in mind to talk to Maestro that very morning about her conversion. She was so eager for him to understand. She started to explain it to him, but he stopped her before she could get going.

He shook his head, "Cara, whatever you now believe, it's all right with me. But don't be so foolish as to try and persuade *me*. I never want to hear about it. We'll only end up shouting at each other, and we need all the energy we have to transform Norma into Brunnhilde. Opera is the only thing we talk about."

"Maestro," Jane said in surprise, "you sound as if you thought I was going to give up opera because of

117

my ..." she tried again, "because I'm now a...." She began a third time, "Maestro, I'm not giving up opera. I've no more thought of giving it up than...." Once more she searched for the right word, this time it came, "... than eating!" She laughed loudly. Maestro laughed too, and the tense moment was over.

"Come, let's have a cup of coffee." He looked at his watch, "We just have time before I meet Mary. Don't sing this week. You gave everything you had last night. It will be good for you to rest your voice and to set your mind to singing Wagner." He made a typical Italian gesture of indifference, "I wish I could like Wagner the way you do. To me he's just loud and long; but honest man that I am, you are the perfect Brunnhilde with your excellent technique in bel canto, your stature, your big voice and insane passion for Wagner."

The next day after Jane had gone over in detail the Brunnhilde score and was sitting alone in her room reading her Bible, or trying to read her Bible, she was thinking how she wished she knew a way to study the Scriptures which was more effective than the method she was pursuing.

"I'll go spend these days with the Schaeffers," she said out loud. "They told me to come back any time and I can return in person all these books I've borrowed." She jumped to her feet, immediately phoned to find out the next train to Aigle, and then placed a call to Switzerland to tell her friends she was coming, that is, if they had room for her and time to answer a few questions. Then the thought of sitting on a sunny balcony breathing in fresh, cool air rather appealed to her too.

22
Like a Sponge

The missionaries had "room and time" for the opera singer, and within twenty-four hours she was sitting on one of the balconies of Chalet les Melezes in full sunshine enjoying the spectacular view and the fresh, clean air. Again Jane was unable to find words to describe the beauty around her. She tried to find the psalm which speaks of the mountains and hills breaking forth into singing and the trees of the fields clapping their hands, and another psalm about the heavens declaring the glory of God and the firmament showing His handiwork. She put down the Bible, but made a mental note to begin memorizing Scripture, and then she simply sat looking, marveling and giving thanks to the One Who made all of it.

Her attention was drawn from the mountains, trees and sky to the field below where a small boy was playing with three goats. The ringing and tinkling of their bells was the masterstroke for which Switzerland is famous. As if what you see is not enough, there is music too. From then on Jane could never look at a picture of Switzerland without hearing it too.

Mrs. Schaeffer had promised to join her as soon as she finished washing the sheets, taking medicine to Susan, putting the dinner in the oven, setting rolls for high tea, writing an urgent letter and welcoming unexpected visitors. When she finally came and before she could sink into a chair, the new convert was ready with her list of questions.

"First I want to know how you read the Bible and second...."

"Jane, PLEASE let me catch my breath!" Edith Schaeffer said laughing. She had never met anyone so direct and positive. "Let me just sit a minute. I've been running all morning."

The impulsive one looked at her friend with genuine remorse and said, "I'm terribly sorry. I should have been helping. I forgot how much of the work you do yourself."

"No, no, no," Edith said quickly. "I didn't mean that." She took a deep breath, "Now I'm fine. All right, let's have that question again, but one at a time, please!"

"Well, now that I've started to read the Bible, I want to know how you read it. It all seems so real to you, and I want it to be just as real to me."

"Hmmmmmmm, no one has asked me that before," Edith said as she paused in her "listening" way which had intrigued the singer from the time they had met.

"You're praying, aren't you?" Jane said abruptly. Before the startled missionary could answer, Jane said with satisfaction, "Aha! Part of your secret is calling on God for everything, little things as well as big, isn't it?"

Edith Schaeffer nodded her head while smiling; she enjoyed the exuberant opera star. "Yes, you're right," she answered, "I was praying. Through years of experience I have learned that God does help and guide me when I ask, so I keep asking!"

"I'll try to explain my approach," she said, while Jane began writing energetically in a notebook, "but remember, I don't pretend this is the only method, or even the best method, but it has made the Bible

120

interesting to me. First, I always read something from both the Old and New Testament. They need to be seen in relationship. A person misses a good deal if he concentrates only on the New Testament, or on devotional books."

She looked at Jane, "Now, don't write down that I said you mustn't read devotional books. The point is, don't read only books about the Bible. Read them *and* the Bible."

She continued, "Then every day I try also to read a psalm. This gives a balanced diet. Then the second point, I read and pray at the same time."

"What was that?" Jane looked up from her note-taking. "You better show me."

"All right, let's open our Bibles to Psalm 27, for example. I was reading it early this morning. Now, and this is important, *before* I read even the first word, I ask the Holy Spirit to cause me to understand the passage I'm about to read. This is vital."

She continued very seriously, "I don't think many of us today sufficiently take into consideration how clouded our minds are, how influenced we are by the anti-Christian world spirit which pours over us through TV, movies, books, paintings and music. How powerful and deceitful Satan is. Sin is very real, Jane, and as you continue to show your intention to go on in a truly Christian way, you'll find that your life will not be easy. Well," she said with a short laugh, "we won't go into *that* today! What I'm trying to stress is the great need every believer in Christ has for the Spirit to continually enlighten and teach us God's truth. A lot of people who read the Bible simply take from it what they want to know. We, as Christians, are to receive from the Scriptures what God wants us to know."

She took a deep breath, and so did Jane, "Now back to Psalm 27—so after I've prayed, I read the first few words: 'The Lord is my light and salvation,' with only

121

those two thoughts I'm ready to pray again! Often very simply, only, 'Thank You, Lord, for being my light and salvation,' and other times it directs me into a long time of praying."

The singer was listening intently. A smile broke on her face and she said, "I think I get it, and I like it. The day I read the same words, I might pray, 'Dear Lord, it seems dark to me in Milan. Be Thou a light unto me and remind me of my salvation.'"

"Yes, excellent, that's the point," Mrs. Schaeffer nodded. "These are living words. The Bible always has something to say, whatever our mood, whoever we are and wherever we are. Take the next brief passage: 'Whom shall I fear?' These four words have pulled me through more emergencies than I'd care to list, and have drawn me into prayer rather than allowing my mind to spin in an endless circle of worrying."

Much more was said that day, and before Edith Schaeffer rushed down to rescue the dinner from the smoking oven, she added one last thing, "My prayer for you, Jane, is that you learn to pray, and that through praying you learn to know God."

The singer soaked up the suggestions given to her like a sponge, and it wasn't surprising that at the dinner table the conversation got back to Bible study and prayer.

23
Concentrate On God

When all the guests, helpers and the Schaeffer family were seated in the Melezes' dining room, it was a tight fit. After the prayer and the serving of the homemade soup, Edith said to Jane, "Before we talk about another thing, I'm dying to know about your performance at Monza the other night?"

Debby added, "We were all praying for you."

"I could tell it," Jane smiled brightly. "There was something different. I don't want to brag, but it was the best singing I've ever done. Maestro ..." Jane laughed as she threw up her hands, "I've never seen Maestro so excited, and if you knew Maestro, he's a man of few words when it comes to praising a performer, but at Monza he was ecstatic with praise. It was a great experience," very sincerely she added, "and I know it was the Lord. There's no other explanation. Believe me, I was praying too, and something else happened that's never happened before. It was my first time on the stage without being a snarling bundle of nerves. Naturally I was tense and keyed up, you *have* to be, or you wouldn't sing with any feeling, but I didn't swear like I used to," with a twinkle in the eye, "Well, maybe a little bit! The things that go on behind the scenes—well, don't get me started on that!"

"What about Maestro, Jane?" Mr. Schaeffer asked. "Remember, you told us you dreaded telling him you had become a Christian."

"Well," she paused, "I'm not sure, but I hope it's going to be all right. At least he knows it now. He refused to talk about it, but I think we understand each other." Passionately she continued, "I can't begin to tell you what a great teacher he is, and a great man. You'd love him. If it wasn't for him and my mother, I'd probably still be singing in a chorus or church choir. I never, never could have got on the stage by myself." She shook her head and went on candidly, "When it comes to opera, Maestro is a genius. This is no exaggeration. He does not miss a thing. Like the other night—suddenly an incense vase on the stage started pouring fumes in my direction while I was singing the 'Casta Diva.' There wasn't a thing I could do. I was in agony, and if it had continued a second longer, I would have coughed in the middle of my aria. Maestro saw exactly what was happening, and got to the vase before the stagehand."

They talked for some time about Jane's career, because, as Debby said, none of them had sat at a table with "a real, live opera star," but it was Jane herself who directed the conversation back to the subject of how to study the Bible.

She said, in the course of thanking the Schaeffers for all the books they had loaned her, "Since I've been reading about Amy Carmichael, Borden of Yale, Hudson Taylor and all the others, it certainly is clear that they knew their Bibles, and I get the impression from them and from you that even a person like myself could get more out of the Bible if I knew how to read it." With a short laugh, she added, "As you all know I'm not the *least* interested in being a teacher or missionary or *something*, as opera is my life, but the way I see it, if I'm willing as an opera singer to spend years trying to understand Wagner, as a Christian I should be willing to give a few hours to the Bible. I did enjoy the Bible studies you sent me, but now I want to know more!"

"Well," said Edith, "to go back to our talk on the balcony. Remember how I was trying to tell you about reading and praying together?"

Jane nodded.

"You see what's so wonderful about the system—and many Christians use it—is that it permits you to pray with the actual words of God," Edith explained. "And there's one other thing I didn't have time to tell you and I thought about afterwards in the kitchen. It's hard to explain, and difficult to learn, and I don't do it every time, but I try to aim my prayer in a Godward direction, and not simply, over and over, recite to the Lord a list of my needs."

She said quickly, "Obviously, because life is made up of a lot of emergencies, quite a few prayers are urgent requests to God for help. I'm sure the Lord understands. I try in my prayer time to concentrate on the majesty of God, His holiness and glory, the mystery and marvel of the Trinity. It's pure delight," the large eyes sparkled, "to just spend time praising God for His creation and His creativity."

In the next few days of her vacation the opera singer tried hard to show her thankfulness to her missionary friends by helping to hand out sheets, drying stacks of dishes and breaking a few while showing Frankie how Brunnhilde holds up her shield. She also mopped a floor or two, using an entire bottle of Ajax on one of them. In between chores, she tried putting into practice reading the Bible while praying.

Before she went down from the mountain she arranged with Mr. Schaeffer to come to Milan to give a Bible study to a group of her friends, and when she walked down the steps to catch the mountain postal bus, Frankie and Debbie had to help with her luggage. Again she borrowed a suitcase of books which had been mentioned in conversations, and in her hand she had the address of the Moody Bible Institute Correspondence School in Chicago.

Jane had spent her last afternoon in the bedroom of Susan, who, shortly after the conversion of the opera singer, had been forced into bed with rheumatic fever. She sat spellbound as the fourteen-year-old girl spoke with animation about the reality of Heaven. Jane had never thought about Heaven as a real place before.

Susan said spontaneously when she saw how interested Jane was in what they were talking about, "Why don't you take some correspondence courses, Jane. You can study in between operas." Then sounding very much like her mother, she said, "I highly recommend Moody's. It's a very sound school."

The train trip back to Milan went quickly as Jane read and prayed through Psalm 27. For two weeks after her return to Italy she had to give her full attention to opera, but no matter how late it was at night she managed to read her Bible and pray. One evening she ran into a snag in Leviticus, it didn't make any sense at all. Suddenly she remembered Susan's advice and immediately wrote for the course, *Introduction to the Whole Bible* and scratched across the bottom of her card, "Please send air mail."

24
"Ho-Jo-To-Ho"

There is something contagious about a person in love with a new idea. The fact that one opera singer had discovered that God is not dead, but is very much alive in the last half of the twentieth century, even in Milan, could not be hid under a wig and costume, even if Jane had tried to. But she didn't hide what she had seen and heard. Early in June Maria Theresa and Georgia went out of town and they asked Jane to teach the class. In a letter to the Schaeffers she described the experience. "The subject was rather difficult, being about the mystery of the indwelling Christ. We all entered into the discussion and afterwards I asked each member to say a short prayer. The meeting lasted until twelve-thirty, so it was lively enough, even though it was the first time I'd done anything like this! I feel the Lord was with us...."

A short time later, Jane's friend Lorna, a British girl married to an Italian, also became a Christian. They decided to teach the Bible class together. They spent hours preparing. When they led the study, within less than ten minutes they had exhausted their knowledge! This prompted Jane to send express letters to the Schaeffers urging them to come to Milan and help.

The opera singer and Lorna continued to speak with anyone who would listen about their conversion and quite a few listened. And so, in the middle of the summer, when Dr. Schaeffer was able to come and speak to the group, mostly made up of opera singers, artists and writers, he did not speak in an empty room. Conspicuously absent was Maestro. He held firmly to what he had told Jane the day they spoke of her religious experience, and she had refrained from talking to him about the explosive subject. But one day, after a brilliant lesson, and Maestro was in a light mood, Jane drew out of her large pocketbook a Bible and asked him to accept it as a present from her. He was furious. His face grew red. He was inwardly seething, and with great effort he took the book and put it on the table, then turned and walked swiftly to the door and stood tensely waiting for his pupil to pass through.

Sharply he said, "Hurry up, Jane. Mrs. Rolandi has our coffee poured, and I detest cold coffee."

Maestro was quite sure that Jane's religious fervor was a passing thing and that if all her friends would ignore her "exhibitionism," as he called it, it would blow over like a gusty Italian storm over Lake Maggiore. He had nothing to complain about her music. Although he was working with her only part-time, as he had placed her in the hands of a Wagnerian conductor for the summer, he was happy with the way her voice was developing and excited about her acting technique which was beginning to be convincing.

At the same time, though, Maestro was haunted with a fear that he did not have her as completely under control now as before. He had a sickening feeling that she had already begun to serve two gods.

It was unfortunate for Maestro's nervous system that he could not have read a letter his star pupil had written to Dr. Schaeffer in June, 1956. It might have encouraged him to learn that he was wrong. (Not the first paragraph, but the second.)

"We do thank you for bringing to us the Word of God on Tuesday evening and awakening even more the spirit that seems to grow daily in our class. We know how tiring a trip like that can be, but this kind of strong, pure faith is so needful here, and most especially in the music world that I pray that you will return to us soon.

"As to the question of 'Should Being a Christian Interfere With An Artist's Career?' I do hope that you will consider it carefully next time, as it is something many will ask. Without yet knowing much I would most assuredly say that being a Christian should be an immense practical and spiritual help to one's career. It is not possible for everyone to be a religious worker; so when an actress (or writer) becomes a Christian, this glorious new power, vision and guidance from God should make that particular artist far, far better. He now has a certain inner quietness, a sense of direction and faith.

"Don't you think that just as our Lord has called some to the pulpit, some to foreign missions, Bach to write music, Rembrandt to paint, He has called others to act or write or sing? Surely those who have Jesus in their hearts have unending possibilities to give from God to others...."

Drinking large amounts of her own philosophy, Jane sang the difficult call of the Valkyrie, "Ho-Jo-To-Ho" with such abounding enthusiasm in practice sessions, singers and teachers in nearby studios were forced to stop and listen. One professor said to another aspiring Wagnerian soprano, "That's the way to sing Wagner!"

Jane was in love with living that summer. Even hot, crowded Milan seemed like a marvelous place to be. Edith wrote, "I hope you are planning to come to

L'Abri again soon, Jane. The roses are in bud, we are eating lettuce, onions and radishes from the garden. The peas look vigorous and other plants progressing. You must come and taste! You know you are more than welcome at any time."

But the energetic and noble Brunnhilde was devoting every waking moment that summer to becoming an interpreter of Wagner that opera lovers would have a hard time forgetting. She had no time for Switzerland. Besides the hours of singing, acting and the continual working on her Italian, she had little time for reading, and as Wagner's philosophy is so important to his music she was forced to use her time of prayer and meditation to study Wagner.

The Moody Bible course arrived, but it was tossed into a drawer. In August she auditioned and immediately received a contract to sing the role of Venus in Wagner's opera *Tannhäuser* in Palermo, where she had had such successful *Turandot* performances several years before.

Cablegrams, letters and telephone calls started coming from the States and elsewhere inviting the young singer to go on tour, to appear on TV, to sing over the radio, to audition in Chicago, at the Met and at other important theaters. What a stimulating time it was, and in spite of the unmerciful heat, about which everyone complained bitterly, that is, everyone who was still in Milan. Most of the people were at the Mediterranean or in the mountains until it cooled off, but Jane did not slacken her pace. The more she perspired, the harder she worked. She always enjoyed losing a few pounds. Signora Rolandi was beside herself, "Darling, you will kill yourself."

Jane's lessons were no longer a torture, because her new faith had given her the one thing she lacked—confidence. Also her lessons were more pleasant, because her voice was now placed, and the main thing was to keep singing, and that she was singing mostly Wagner's music which she had dreamed about doing since childhood. It was an intoxicating time. It was that ineffably grand feeling of being on the verge of something marvelous that was soon to take place.

The young Christian, without discussing it with anyone, felt certain that she must be experiencing "fullness of joy." She had read about it in one of the Christian books that the Schaeffers had loaned her in the springtime. It was like the feeling one gets early in May when the sharp, rude air becomes gentle overnight, and the only possible mood is joy. She couldn't imagine that she would ever be unhappy again in her life. Her joy had no beginning nor end. It was simply there. She was a bit bothered with some "older" Christians she knew who seemed to have problems in their lives. Why couldn't they be as happy as she was?

And then with absolutely no warning, no sounding of gongs, the air around her became charged with fiery darts. She tried running, ducking, laughing, shouting, but Satan's angels are expert marksmen at shooting down the self-satisfied Christian. For the first time as a child of Gòd, the opera singer personally experienced Paul's lament, "For the good that I would I do not: but the evil which I would not, that I do." She was shocked to learn that as an "experienced" Christian of five months she was more vulnerable to sin than ever, and how extra cruel to be attacked where she thought she had had complete victory. Everything fell apart at once, and to add to her disappointment in herself and her disillusion in her faith, she had several unpleasant scenes with her best friends who began picking on her. Finally they had had enough of her pious words.

One day they were all having dinner at Signora Rolandi's, something they had not done all summer because people had been out of town, and also because now Maestro and Mary had their own apartment. At the beginning of the meal Jane had bowed her head to pray. This was too much for her friends.

"Now look at her," one of them taunted. "Always showing off! Always pretending she's so much better than we are! Always got answers! Always praying! You better pray for yourself, sinner. We're not so impressed with your piety...." They let her have it hard.

Jane tried to be silent, but the gibes continued to fall. Almost in tears, she retorted, "I'm not showing off. Simply trying to thank God for this meal."

"It's more to the point to thank Signora Rolandi," another of Maestro's pupils said with a laugh. "She's the one who prepared it."

Abruptly Jane pushed away from the table, mumbling something about "getting a handkerchief," not wishing for them to see her cry. Before she crossed the room, Maestro called after her, "Come back, Salamona! You mustn't take it seriously. We're only teasing you. We...."

In the middle of his words, he jumped to his feet, overturning his chair by mistake, because suddenly he saw Jane double over as she approached the door.

In alarm, he cried, "Jane's sick! Come, help!" as the now all-compassionate, warmhearted friend rushed to catch his beloved pupil before she fainted.

Italian people are not notorious for their calmness in ordinary circumstances, and in an emergency such as this, one well-meaning friend collides, yells at and bumps into other well-meaning friends in their attempts to help the stricken one.

"Mamma mia!" sobbed Signora Rolandi, wringing her hands.

"Cara!" shouted Maestro.

"Bella Salamona!" groaned the friend who had said such mean things to Jane, crossing himself over and over, "Forgive me, forgive me, forgive me!"

"Shut up, all of you!" yelled Mary, who was born and raised in New England, and came into the situation like a Yankee captain leading a troop over a hill, "Let's get her in bed and call the doctor!"

With great difficulty the friends dragged, pulled and lifted the "statuesque" opera singer from the dining room into the bedroom. Signora Rolandi ordered the men out of the room so she could make Jane more comfortable. In the meantime, Mary was talking to the doctor on the telephone. Signora sat by Jane's bedside holding a cool cloth against the burning forehead until her son who was Jane's doctor rushed into the room.

For the first few days the opera singer had a raging temperature, and at one low, unbearable moment, her remorseful friends, who had been standing around scarcely able to do another thing since her illness, even feared for her life. She had a severe and painful case of jaundice, by far the worst illness she had known in her life, and besides the physical agony, the stricken singer was deeply depressed.

She was so ill she couldn't read, couldn't listen to music, couldn't have visitors, and even when she finally began to feel better the doctor still insisted that she remain absolutely quiet and stay in the dark. But the one thing he could not place limits on was her mind and spirit. She shed many bitter tears for her faithlessness to her Lord all summer, for her foolishness, for her pride, and then she agonized over and over about the Brunnhilde performance only a month away, whether or not she'd be able to sing.

Every day the doctor came to see her, and Maestro and Mary and Signora were wonderfully kind to her, and did everything in their power to help the Bella Salamona get well.

One afternoon, when she was finally able to sit up, and there was a suggestion of a smile on the yellow, drawn face, it was Signora Rolandi who tiptoed into the darkened room with Jane's Bible. "Maybe this will help you get better, cara," she said gently. "What you believe is your business. When we both have more time, you must help me understand what's in that book."

Before she went to sleep that night Jane read and prayed through Psalm 27 beginning with, "The Lord is my light and my salvation; whom shall I fear? the Lord is the strength of my life; of whom shall I be afraid?" to the end, "Wait on the Lord: be of good courage, and He shall strengthen thine heart: wait, I say, on the Lord."

25
A Hot-Blooded Roman

Anyone as basically healthy as Jane is able to make a swift recovery from even a serious illness with the right medicine, a good doctor, lots of loving care and the help of the Lord. Early in October when she was well enough to read again, she began reviewing her opera notes, so as soon as the doctor told her she could sing she would be able to pick up where she left off.

Without discussing it with anyone, the young Christian sensed that the deep depression she experienced during her illness had been, in part, a spiritual battle. It did not shake her faith, rather it made her realize how dependent she was on prayer and study to stay close to God, and that her concept of "fullness of joy" was pathetically shallow. For the first time as a Christian she really humbled herself before her Lord, and in childlike faith asked that He would lead and teach her, and that she would no longer trust in her own theories. From that moment on, the Bible and her correspondence course became her constant companions.

Without her scarcely realizing it, as she began to dig deeper into the teachings of the Bible, she gradually began to take offence at certain procedures in the theatrical world which previously she accepted as routine or normal. One day while reviewing the notes she had taken during the past summer on the role of Tosca, she came on this, "Act I, duet, passionate woman, always the actress. Show all your body. Even your public must be made to desire you. This is a hot-blooded Roman after her man...."

Even early in that summer this would not have bothered Jane. She would have accepted it as part of the profession. An actress is an actress. Her part is to interpret the role as realistically as possible. This is theater, but for the first time the singer had some doubts about this.

Before Jane's conversion she had no standard in her life for morality. Even though she believed there was a God, her personal optimism led her to believe that all religions were good and so, actually, she was in the same position as many today who live without the authority of the Bible in their lives. People without guidelines spend much of their time "shopping around" trying to find a satisfactory way to live which brings them happiness and a sense of fulfillment and purpose. One day they listen to Freud, the next day perhaps it's the essays of Sartre, or they might prefer the teaching of Jung. He taught that a formalized religion was not at all necessary for a person to be integrated or emotionally healthy. All that is needed, he said, is for each person in his own way to make peace with "the unseen and perhaps unknowable power behind creation and the universe."

But for Jane it was a great relief and a help to learn that God *does* have a standard, and that it is as valid today as it was to her Grandfather Wysor, who was a prominent lawyer and noted orator in Southwestern Virginia. She thought of the ancestors on both sides of her family who had come to America because of their great conviction that God's way is the only way.

Shortly after her conversion she wrote in her diary,

"At last I know what is right and wrong," And a few days later, "Sin is anything in thought, word and deed which does not show forth God's character, either His holiness or love."

In puzzling about the advice given to her how to interpret the part of Tosca and at the same time "show forth the holiness of God," Jane was reminded of a violent argument that she had had with her mother over a publicity picture which she had taken in a new costume with a low neckline. When Mrs. Smith saw the picture, she said firmly, "No daughter of mine is going to appear on stage or in print indecently exposed!" And that was the end of that. It had been a big joke among Jane and her opera friends, and Jane had laughed as hard as the others about her mother's "puritan" standards. But in October, 1956, Jane, for the first time, appreciated the moral courage of her mother.

This quandary about how to portray Tosca was one of the first premonitions the singer had that the Lord might have other plans for her life than opera, but immediately she swept the thought from her mind. She laughed loudly when she saw what an easy solution there was to the problem. There are many, many other operas; I simply won't sing Tosca, which turned her mind to Brunnhilde. Of all Wagner's characters Brunnhilde is the most wholesome and noble. That role she could sing in all honesty, well, that is, if she didn't ponder too deeply Wagner's confused, mystical interpretation of Christianity. Back to Brunnhilde she turned with satisfaction and enthusiasm, and soon the sound of the warrior cry, "Ho-Jo-To-Ho" was filling the air.

26
Brunnhilde Goes on Tour

Jane's friend, Kay, an opera lover and an authority on Wagner, had flown from New York City to hear Jane sing and spend some time with her. While they traveled to Sicily for the opening of *La Walkiria* in Catania, Jane entertained her with some of the amusing dramas behind the scenes. Amid the laughter Kay commented, "I wonder what will happen this week!"

The rehearsals went reasonably well, excepting for one incident. The conductor became furious with the Valkyries who play the parts of the sister warriors to Brunnhilde. All of the singers happened to be rather plump (as Maestro said, "A large voice needs a large case. A cello doesn't come in a piccolo frame"). When they finished their part of the singing in the first rehearsal, they all changed their costumes and went out in front to watch the rest of the performance. Wagner's operas are long, some of them very, very long, and the "warriors" saw no reason why they should stand around backstage in their cumbersome costumes when they did not appear again in the performance. But the conductor did not see it that way.

"On opening night," he yelled at the frightened singers, "I want everyone of you to take a curtain call at the end of the performance in full costume."

The night of the gala performance came, and it was a notable success with tremendous applause and acclamation. Because of her excellent technique and dramatic ability, Jane gave to the role of Brunnhilde a flaming nobility, and yet in an appealing, youthful way. There was nothing pompous about her performance. The eight Valkyries sang competently and with spirit too, and, as they had been instructed, at the end of the performance they all filed out for their curtain call.

As they were bowing and smiling, turning this way and that way, and as the clapping increased, they forgot completely how furious they were at the conductor, and were adoring all the attention they were getting. But pride goeth before a fall. Abruptly one of the stouter of the warrior singers disappeared. Completely disappeared from sight. There was an audible gasp from the first few rows in the front of the theater. She had fallen feet first into the prompter's box. As Jane said later, "Fortunately for the prompter, he wasn't there!"

As Kay reported it in the *Opera News*, "It is a sad reflection on her sisters that they simply stood by holding hands, helpless with surprise and laughter, while the unfortunate, but uninjured Valkyrie heaved herself back on to the stage unaided."

And that was the first and last time the Valkyries were invited to participate in a curtain call. But that wasn't the end of the drama behind the drama in Catania.

The night of the third performance of *La Walkiria* was very warm, and the temperature is always even warmer on stage. The bass-baritone singing the role of Wotan was an excellent singer of sizeable proportion. As he was singing to Jane (Brunnhilde) and she was supposed to be looking soulfully into his eyes, she couldn't help noticing how profusely he was perspiring. All of a sudden, a panicky look came into his eyes and he began making exaggerated, twitchy movements with his mouth and nose. Jane thought he was having some sort of attack, but then she realized with horror that he was trying to keep his moustasche in place. Then as he gave his all to hit a high note, first one side of the moustache fluttered off and landed in the middle of his fat stomach, and in a moment the other side joined it, and there, like a butterfly it perched throughout the duet. And as if that was not enough, just as he was finishing his part, Jane noticed that the whole side of his face was slipping! His beard and the patch over his eye was about to fall off. "Help me, help me," he whispered wildly, and so when the two stars embraced, Jane gave him a powerful clap on the cheek and sort of hung on that side of his face hoping to get the beard stuck on again....

It was after that performance that one of the newspaper critics wrote about how much fire and vitality the American soprano from Virginia put into her acting, particularly the duet between Brunnhilde and Wotan!

Jane thoroughly enjoyed the visit to Catania. Besides singing her favorite role, she enjoyed sharing the time in Sicily with a close friend, someone who loved the theater as much as she did. Whenever she was free from rehearsals, she and Kay walked about the streets of the busy seaport. It is a colorful city, and in the background is the dramatic Mt. Etna. Catania was the birthplace of one of Jane's favorite composers, Bellini. And it was a thrill and an honor for her to sing in the Teatro Bellini, the crowning memorial to the great musician. Jane loved singing there, also because of the warm response of the music-loving people and the beauty of the auditorium which rises in five tiers of brilliant red, gold and ivory to the ceiling where there are colorful frescoes of scenes from Bellini operas. The theater has a large, modern stage which can be seen from all parts of the horseshoe-shaped auditorium, and for these performances the management had installed a whole new steam apparatus for the dramatic fire in the last act of *La Walkiria*. Jane looked forward to singing many times in Catania, and she had reason enough to believe she would be asked again from the enthusiastic reception she had received from both the press and the audiences....

The next few months were again given over to hard work preparing for *Tannhäuser*, but she did allow herself a three-day holiday in January to visit in Switzerland, and immediately it was back to opera.

During the second week in February she was in Sicily again, this time in Palermo. As with other artists, Jane had an exacting, critical spirit, particularly about her own singing and acting. If she sang less than her best, it was recorded in her diary. If it was good, she said that. Her aim was always to improve, to learn what she was doing wrong, or right, so the next time she could sing better. When she wrote in her notes after singing the role of Venus in *Tannhäuser* at Palermo, "Very good. Last performances the best I've done. Voice in really fine shape now. Need simply to sing a great deal and make money"—this was not vanity nor greed, but an honest appraisal where she now stood in the opera world.

When one considers the years of hard work, the hours of studying, the expense of costumes and the high cost of living as others would have opera singers live, one can appreciate Jane's genuine excitement at the prospect ahead of her for reward. As a Christian she was thrilled to be earning more money, because that meant she could give more to missions and places where it was needed. Much could be written about the opera singer's generosity. From the day she was converted she started giving to those who were proclaiming the truth so that others might hear, and she gave freely when she didn't have much to give.

After the *Tannhäuser* performances she went to America and the Bible and correspondence course (by this time she was on her third or fourth course) went with her, but she did not have much time for study, nor many opportunities to discuss her new faith with friends and family. They were more interested to hear about her triumphs in opera, and it is hard not to enjoy talking about success. Then, of course, she was in great demand to sing.

Before she left for an extensive concert tour in the South and Middle West, the opera star gave a big cocktail party for her friends in Roanoke. At the party she managed to get into a few discussions about her conversion, but no one paid too much attention to what she said. During these weeks in America she wrote a discouraging letter to Edith Schaeffer intimating that she did not know what was wrong, but hardly anyone listened to her when she spoke about spiritual matters.

It would have been easy (and it was tempting) for the missionary friends to write back, "But Jane, you are hardly living a life that is conducive for spiritual growth. Cocktail parties are not the best pulpits from which to preach." Or they could have written, "Have you considered leaving the opera world?" But not once did the Schaeffers urge her in this direction. How could they know what God wanted for her life? This was His business not theirs. But what they did do was pray for her, and their prayer was that the Holy Spirit would guide her and clearly show her which way to go. What they did recommend was more prayer herself and to go on studying the Word of God. Once Jane started on the tour, she did have occasional quiet times on a train or in a hotel.

In the spring of 1957 she returned to Milan and spent another warm summer there. Before she left for

Munich in the fall to study German and to pursue Wagnerian opera in the language in which it was meant to be sung, she recorded in her diary, "Maestro Verna, 4:30 pm. Dear, wonderful friend. Last lesson for a while."

And little did the Bella Salamona suspect it was one of the last lessons she would ever have with the beloved teacher.

27
Sparks in the Air

Shortly before going to Germany Jane went to Switzerland to sing in the wedding of the Schaeffers' eldest daughter, Priscilla. It was the first time any of them had heard the opera star sing. Mrs. Schaeffer described it in a letter, "Her voice filled the place, we were full of awe as we lost ourselves in the beauty of the music. It was a terrific experience and we all just sighed as she finished. What a wedding gift!"

Dr. Martyn Lloyd-Jones of London performed the ceremony, and later Jane was privileged to talk with the great clergyman. One of the L'Abri friends had told her that formerly he was a successful medical doctor, but he gave up his career to preach the gospel. The story made an impression upon the singer and she thought of what his friends, his associates in the medical profession, must have said. What an agony for him to renounce that for which he had prepared.

Jane's year in Germany was frequently interrupted as she travelled about, mostly in Italy, for opera performances. Because of the many times she was engaged to sing Princess Turandot, she acquired the title *Turandot Internationale*. Her visits to Milan were always difficult. It was the same old conflict. Naturally Jane still had a keen interest in the Bible class which had steadily been growing in number, and always there was at least one unpleasant scene with her opera friends when she telephoned or went to see the Christian friends.

Even though Jane's time in Germany was often lonely (and at first, she was like one living on an island as far as having any spiritual acquaintances), she found it satisfying to return to Munich where she could pray, read her Bible and speak with whomever she wished about her faith. In January, 1958 she wrote to Edith Schaeffer, "...Last night I was invited to a large masked ball which is a specialty in Munich at this time of year, but though it was very lively and the people charming, I kept wishing I could spend those hours with the Lord in prayer and thinking of the power that would have come from it rather than wasted time in foolish, light talk! The Holy Spirit is not letting me alone one minute...."

"Feb 7, 1958, Munich
"My dear Mrs. Schaeffer,
    "What a joy it was to receive the package of books which seemed to have been sent straight from heaven! I have already read the Martin Luther.... My prayers are sent your way every morning and I feel very near the work though mine is no visible work. I continue to feel a pressing need for Milan.... I feel a great work can be done there, but the victory shall be won only through prayer.... I shall be leaving for Palermo in about two weeks as I must be there about the 20th. Who will be teaching the class in Milano on the 18th?...
    "Again thanks for the books and please know how much they mean to me. I have a group ready to mail back to you. I loved the St. John children's book. Where can I order them for my nieces and nephews?"

145

Jane did sing in Palermo, the part of Helen of Troy in *Mephistopheles*, but later she told Mrs. Schaeffer, "It was the sort of performance I would rather forget. I missed Maestro dreadfully. No one prepares me for a role better than he does ... so it wasn't very good. Oh well, on to the next part!" She added, "Not even Flagstad had one hundred per cent triumphs!!"

That year in Germany Jane wrote many letters to Edith Schaeffer, and in going over them I was impressed with two things, no, three. First, her hunger to learn. She was everlastingly writing for more books, and the faithful Schaeffers continued wrapping and mailing them. If for some reason they were slow in coming, she'd reread the ones she had.

Second, she was always sharing her new faith with someone, directly or through the mail. Every member of her family (and Virginia families can be large if you include all the second cousins, great-aunts and those with the same middle name, as, of course, they do) received booklets, tracts, Bible studies, Bibles, books and sermons. And as soon as she learned a few words in German, she was speaking to those around her about the Lord.

In April she moved into a new "pension," and in another letter to Mrs. Schaeffer she wrote, "I am now in a new home and am most delighted with it. The people who live here apparently are very aristocratic, but lost their son during the war. The home is beautiful and filled with amazing antiques and paintings. There are about six younger people living here and how my heart burns to talk to them of the Lord. Please continue praying as I need it in a very special way at this time. If only we could remember not to get lost in the things of the hour, but long for the things eternal...."

A third thing was noticeable in Jane's letters. Her life did not run along in a valley, like a trolley car on a track. It was more like a roller coaster, with exciting highs and a few distressing lows. One letter reported, "I'm reading a long series of sermons given by Dr. Martyn Lloyd-Jones on the 'Sermon on the Mount' which are very, very fine, though I've had such a difficult time spiritually in the last month that just in these days I feel I've lost some of the reality, and at times feel I'm just reading things out of books. These verses keep returning to me even during the night, I Corinthians 3:11-15, 'For other foundation can no man lay than that is laid, which is Jesus Christ. Now if any man build upon this foundation gold, silver, precious stones, wood, hay, stubble; every man's work shall be made manifest: for the day shall declare it, because it shall be revealed by fire; and the fire shall try every man's work of what sort it is. If any man's work abide which he hath built thereupon, he shall receive a reward. If any man's work shall be burned, he shall suffer loss: but he himself shall be saved: yet so as by fire.' If the Lord wants to do a work through me then I do ask your prayers that I myself be willing. The wretchedness of sin that causes us to walk our narrow, little way when the Lord has chosen such unending riches for those who love Him and walk in His wonderful ways."

Again it was a foreshadow that the mind of the opera singer was beginning to hear another call, but her heart and will refused to believe it, because her whole life, and so many other lives, were wrapped up in opera.

"July 15, 1958, Munich

"...I have just finished reading about one hundred sermons of Dr. Martyn Lloyd-Jones. And they have somewhat shaken me up and caused me to doubt my salvation which I don't want to do, but also driven me to longing for a more Christian life. Do you have any books on Henry Martyn and John Fletcher who he mentions so often? I have almost run out of books, and would appreciate it ever so much if you could send on a few more. Tonight I finished my fifth exam of the Moody Bible course—it necessarily goes a bit slower as I am reading the Bible in German...."

(While in Italy she always read her Bible in Italian, a bit slower also, but it helps to explain Jane's proficiency in several languages today.)

In September Jane went to Austria to study with a professor in Graz whom Maestro had recommended. While she was there, she received a letter from Roanoke inviting her to sing in the *Messiah* when she would be home in Virginia for Christmas. And so along with reading the *Screwtape Letters*, doing another correspondence course which was supposed to take three months, but which she finished in three days, and studying for two operas, she began memorizing the soprano parts for the *Messiah*.

"Sep. 16, 1958, Graz
"...a large German Bible should arrive any day at the chalet as I imagine you have Germans now and then and might need an extra copy. Notice Luther's translation of the Apocrypha.

"Am thrilled to be going to Athens soon and can hardly wait to stand on Mars Hill where St. Paul addressed the Athenians. I remember visiting there before, but then it meant nothing. Oh, the joy of being born into God's family. Shall stop in Milan on the way and hope to be at Bible class Tuesday."

In the same letter to Edith Schaeffer she scribbled this P.S., "Received a letter from your father concerning books for young people. Can you also give suggestions? I have all ages of nieces and nephews from 15 on down...."

Around this time Jane complained in one of the

letters to Mrs. Schaeffer that the Lord wasn't giving her much light, that it wasn't at all clear to her what He wanted her to do, and a letter came back to her suggesting that she read Isaiah 50, verses 10 and 11, "Who is among you that feareth the Lord, that obeyeth the voice of his servant, that walketh in darkness, and hath no light? Let him trust in the name of the Lord, and stay upon his God. Behold, all ye that kindle a fire, that compass yourselves about with sparks: walk in the light of your fire, and in the sparks that ye kindled. This shall ye have of mine hand; ye shall lie down in sorrow."

The opera singer went into a rage when she read these words, not against her missionary friend but against God and the flaming brightness of His words. She shook her fist, she sniffed, snorted and stamped about the room while shouting shrilly, "I will not! I shall not! You can't make me, God!"

The sudden dreadful outburst which seemed to come out of not much at all, illustrated vividly what a battlefield Jane's heart had already become over the issue of whether opera was the Lord's choice for her life. The next letter to the Schaeffers helps to explain what a desperate struggle was going on in the soul of the converted opera star. Her hours of Bible study, the praying, the reading of the best in Christian literature had pressed home to her the truth that no servant can serve two masters. It was a terrible scene, and if Maestro would have witnessed it he would have said, "Save it for the stage. Wagner wrote for a possessed woman like you!"

But this was not the theater, the world of make-believe. It was a life-and-death, supernatural struggle going on between the real God Who is there and one of His rebellious creatures. Almost immediately after Jane had shouted angrily against God she was on her face in tears begging forgiveness. If

149

there is one thing that proves whether or not a person honestly believes God *is* there, it is his reverential respect for Him. One of the Proverbs says, "The fear of the Lord is the beginning of wisdom." Jane was not only humiliated and shocked at her outburst against the Living God, but she feared Him.

After a sobering time of prayer, the singer wrote a confidential letter to the Schaeffers which clearly revealed the silent warfare which was going on behind the facade of the successful and happy opera star which her public knew. "On this separate page I shall put down on paper what I have not said to anyone but the Lord, and ask that it go no further than you and Dr. Schaeffer for the time being. Your last letter with the Isaiah quotation made me furious as it struck a tender spot. People continually ask me if my 'new interest' is not interfering with my career which I stormily answer, 'NO!'—but there is not inner rest over the matter.

"On August 1st I told the Lord I would go on in opera one more year, and prayed that if He were truly my Father in heaven He would make it clear to me, in my heart as well as in my mind, if He would have me continue in this way, or another, according to His will. I feel that He has given me the assurance that I am to sing, but where and what, I don't know. An opera career is certainly my Isaac, and I cannot seem to put it on the fire.

"It is absolutely overwhelming to me that Abraham could do such a thing in all serenity. Don't you think certain people are given a special gift of faith?" she asked hopefully. "Mine seems to fade at the first cloud in the sky. One thing is certain; something has taken possession of my life which I cannot deny. I do beg of you to pray with me that the Lord may work this year in such a way as to make His will very clear, and what is far more important, that He will work in my heart that I will want His will more than anything in life (it is an impossible task which only the Lord can manage)...."

At the end of the letter she wrote, "The Christian life is not roses and pink clouds, as some 'spiritual' books would have us think...."

28
Mars Hill

It was headline news all over Virginia: "GREEK ROYALTY TO HEAR ROANOKER IN OPERA!" Everything about the trip to Athens was a reporter's delight. She not only sang brilliantly and impressed the Athenians with her majestic stage presence, but again she charmed those who met her with the warmth of her personality.

She and Signora Rolandi had a wonderful time in between rehearsals and performances being entertained and taken on tours in and near the famous city. For Jane it was a solemn experience to stand on Mars Hill and to recall the Apostle Paul's words to the Greeks and foreigners who regularly gathered there to hear some new thing.

In an interview over the radio Jane was asked what was the high point of her visit in Athens. She replied, "Standing on Mars Hill and remembering Paul's words to the Athenians as he looked towards the beautiful Acropolis 'God that made the world and all things therein, seeing that he is Lord of heaven and earth, dwells not in temples made with hands....' "

A day later as Signora and Jane were sitting on the deck of the Turkish boat as it glided past the coastline of Greece with its occasional clusters of columns or a lone temple standing on a barren hill silhouetted against the blue sky. Startling white villages fitted into the rocky hills. They were going over the reviews of the performances. They were in Greek, of course, but a friend had thoughtfully had them translated into English, and Jane was attempting to translate the extravagant praise into Italian for Signora, who kept clasping her hands together and murmuring, while tears rolled down her cheeks as always when very happy, "Bella Salamona, cara mia, o, gioia!"

Finally Jane threw down the stack of papers on the deck and yawned loudly, "Even I get fed up with hearing how wonderful I am after a while!"

She laughed in a spirited way, and a sailor who was up at the top of a ladder near them echoed her laughter.

Signora picked up her knitting and Jane excused herself to go get something in their stateroom. Before she left the deck she stopped and looked at the water, sometimes turquoise, sometimes blue. She watched in fascination, because it seemed as if the glowing sun was shining up through the water, like the "living water" spoken of in the book of John. For the first time she could picture how it works. The sun isn't in the water, she thought. It just appears as if it is. She ran to the stateroom to find that verse, and when she did, she read it through several times, "He that believeth on Me, out of his inner life shall flow rivers of living water."

Jane's next letter to Mrs. Schaeffer came again from Graz in Austria, dated October 17th, 1958, "At last I'm back in Austria after a lovely trip by boat to Venice. We landed just at sunset, and you can imagine the breathtaking splendor! The Lord was overwhelmingly generous to me in Athens, and the big success (the best I have ever had) was all His doing...."

The rest of the letter was filled with excitement over the news that Dorothy (the same Dot who had been helping the Schaeffers on Jane's first visit to the chalet)

153

and her minister-husband Hurvey felt called to move to Milan and carry on the work of L'Abri there.

After Athens the singer continued to study two or three operas and the *Messiah*, to work on German, to study the Bible, to spend time in the art museums and to talk on the telephone with Mary, Maestro and Signora. According to Signora, Maestro would say every once in a while, "Let's call Bella Salamona and see how she is."

Jane worked hard on learning German. It is not enough for an opera singer to know a few words in the languages she sings, she must become fluent, not only to sing the opera, but in order to understand the conductor, the stagehands and the others involved in a production. She had sung the role of Brunnhilde at Catania in Italian, now she was learning the part in German, and many things in "Ho-Jo-To-Ho" and elsewhere, needed relearning. When her teacher told the singer to think of the call as a yodel, suddenly it came out of the Virginian freely. Those who had lived in Jane's neighborhood when she was a child wearing a cowboy suit with guns on her hips knew that she had a powerful voice, because she and her friend, Whittle, used to signal to one another with a special yodel which could be heard for blocks.

In November on her way to America, she planned to meet the Schaeffers in England where Dr. Schaeffer was speaking to students from Oxford and Cambridge, but first she flew to Munich and then to Frankfurt to discuss with her agent several new contracts. Before she left she wrote to Mrs. Schaeffer, "Thrilled to be seeing you soon. Yes, thank you so much for the books which I read almost as soon as they arrived and mailed back three days later. *Mimosa* was deeply touching and the Thomas Lambie book a great inspiration.... Am working hard on the *Messiah* which I look forward to singing more than anything I've ever sung."

29
Telephones Start Ringing

Jane's time in England was a good preparation for her Christmas visit at home. As she looked around the crowded room at the intelligent, eager, occasionally belligerent faces, she was fascinated with the speed in which they asked questions of Dr. Schaeffer and the skillful way he answered. And when the climax to a point was reached it was always the pure, strong words of Scripture that were the final authority.

In a few days, when she arrived in Roanoke, Jane was met by photographers and reporters. They questioned her about the Athens appearance, how long she'd be in town, and the location of her next performance. In the interview she mentioned how thrilled she was to be singing in the *Messiah*, which led to questions about her conversion.

When Jane saw the paper the following day she was happily surprised to note that a whole paragraph was devoted to her spiritual awakening while visiting in the Swiss Alps in 1956. A number of other people read the same article, and telephones started ringing, particularly among the members of the Wednesday Morning Bible Study, a very alive Christian group in Roanoke taught by two dedicated teachers, Roberta Renner and Mrs. Tanner.

"Did you see the article about Jane Stuart Smith?" Bettie asked her sister, Dorothy. "It sounds as if she *really* has been converted!"

"Yes, I read it three times. We better call Roberta. This is wonderful."

And before Dorothy could call Roberta, the phone rang. "Hello, Dorothy. This is Roberta. Have you read the paper this morning?"

Several members of the class got together, and after prayer decided Dorothy should be the one to call the opera star. The telephone conversation began stiffly, and Dorothy was at a loss what to say next. Jane was not over-friendly because she thought it was another of the tiresome calls which people whose names frequently appear in the news often have to endure. In a trembling voice Dorothy referred to the article in the paper and said something about believing God....

"Are you a real Christian too?" boomed out the singer. And then she laughed in a loud, contagious way which nearly unseated Dorothy at the other end of the line. Now very friendly, she said, "I didn't mean it *quite* the way it sounded. It's possible half the people in Roanoke are Christians but what *is* hard for me to understand is how can they be so casual about it. I mean, I think it's something to be excited about, don't you?"

Dorothy agreed, and the conversation flowed on as if the two had been friends for years. Within a day or two Roberta called and invited Jane to speak to the Wednesday Bible class. And on the following Wednesday morning as the opera singer spoke simply, and yet with power, about the wonder of God's love and concern for people by sending His only Son to redeem them from their sins, the rivers of living water flowed into the hearts of several others, including Jane's beloved sister-in-law, Liggie. This was the beginning of many wonderful, miraculous

156

happenings, abiding friendships and spiritual richness which could fill another book, a thick book.

Singing in the *Messiah* was a deep, spiritual experience for Jane and for many who heard it, and soon the visit in Roanoke was over. On the first of January she flew to Bari in the southern part of Italy, where she sang Turandot. One quotation from the newspaper, *Il Secolo d'Italia,* January 8th, 1959, will indicate how she was received:

> The triumph of the evening were the soprano Jane Stuart Smith and the tenor Mario Filippeschi, as well as the conductor Angelo Questa.
>
> Jane Stuart Smith was for Bari a new name although preceded by merited fame as she came from the school of Ettore Verna and has already had great successes in the theaters of Venice, Palermo, as well as others.
>
> The Bari public, which enjoys the merited fame of connoisseurs of value, after a polite wait, burst into enthusiastic applause....

By the middle of January she was in London again, this time for auditioning. She made a wonderful discovery while she was roaming around London. She learned about the Evangelical Library with branches in many parts of the world, but what was of immediate interest to her (and to Edith Schaeffer, who must have spent hours wrapping and sending books to Jane), they had a lending library, and for a small fee would mail books to any place in the world. They soon discovered that a certain Miss Jane Stuart Smith was very interested in sound, Christian literature. Also in London, she was thrilled to get notes from two nieces and nephews telling of their new love for the Bible.

Instead of going back to Munich from England she went to Vienna, because Maestro wanted her to have experience in the Vienna Opera House, and also he felt it important for her to be in the same city with her new manager.

She located a delightful "pension" on the main street of Vienna with her windows overlooking the Opera House. Across from the dining room there was a charming sitting room, and the singer's first thought—a perfect place for a Bible class.

In Jane's first meeting with the new manager he handed her a contract to sing *Die Walküre* in German in Naples. Career-wise this was another step up the ladder of success.

30
A Castle Crumbles in Vienna

"**E**xcuse me," said the tall young man with a cane, "but I have seen you here on several occasions, and you always seem to be puzzling over this painting. I too am interested in Breughel."

Jane looked to see who was speaking to her and noticed that the stranger had a kind, but sad, face.

"I'd be thankful if you could help me understand what Breughel is trying to say," she said frankly. "He has placed Christ in the center of the teeming culture of people, but He is almost lost in the crowd."

"It's only my personal theory," the gentleman said, "but I feel Breughel is trying to say that Christ is not unimportant, but it's the people in all their nervous activity that make Him seem insignificant."

"Ah," said the singer. "I like that. I'll have to think about it."

She smiled in appreciation. This led to a stimulating conversation between the two strangers who had a common interest in painting, particularly Breughel. In their talking, Jane learned that Hans was an architect and Austrian and that he had been injured in the war and that he was an agnostic. He learned that Jane was an opera singer, American, had a hearty and exuberant outlook on life and was a Christian.

"If you'd like, Miss Smith," he said, "we can look at some of these other paintings together."

The large room was full of Breughel.

"Fine," she said, "I appreciate your willingness to take time. I really am interested in his paintings."

As it turned out, Hans had lots of time for the opera singer during her stay in Vienna.

Jane, while in Munich, had started to translate into German Mr. Schaeffer's Basic Bible Studies but it was an impossible task for her. What a relief to find Hans, who was not only willing to correct her many mistakes in grammar, but willing to go ahead with the translation, providing they would do it together.

And so the winter months passed pleasantly enough, on the surface at least, although inwardly Jane was reaching the storm warning signal.

One night in April, when Hans and Jane were again working on the translation, he asked, "Why haven't you been to the opera recently, Jane? When I first met you, you used to go often."

She paused, and then said the most surprising thing, "I don't enjoy opera any more!"

"As you Americans say, 'Are you kidding?' " asked Hans.

"No," she said with a funny laugh, "I don't enjoy it any more. It's uncanny. I can't understand what's happening to me." She stopped and seemed to weigh in her mind whether or not to say any more, but she seemed to need to say it to someone, and so she went on, "I haven't told this to a soul, but about two weeks ago, when you had to work that night and I went to *Tristan and Isolde,* I ran out of the theater after the second act!" She rushed on speaking with deep feeling, "I'm sure people thought I was ill or crazy. I nearly was both, but the most deadly feeling of boredom had come over me. I couldn't bear to sit in the theater another minute!"

160

Hans stared at the floor. He was aware what opera meant to her, and he knew for her to be talking this way was highly irregular. He didn't have the courage to look at the singer now on the verge of tears.

He pushed back his chair awkwardly, "I'll get some coffee."

"Yes, yes," Jane sniffled. "That's what I'd love, a strong cup of coffee."

When Hans returned, she sipped the coffee and soon continued the story, only now with more composure, "I ran back here and threw myself on my bed and dissolved in tears. I kept thinking—my castle in the sky has crumbled. But I think I'm understanding it now, Hans. For the first time I dared to look at opera with open eyes, and I saw it clearly. I can't stand on a stage playing the part of an adulteress and then go and tell people to believe in Christ because He can change their lives. He has to completely change my life before it will be convincing to others." She said, close to tears again, "I could walk out on opera right this minute. The Lord has really changed my taste, but," and she pounded the table with her fist, "I haven't the courage to quit. How can I tell Maestro, how can I tell my parents, what about all the people...."

Finally her voice trailed off, she hated making a scene in front of Hans, in front of anyone, "Most of all I can't stand hurting my mother and Maestro. Hans, if you knew how hard they've worked and how excited they are with all the possibilities ahead ... but something is going to have to happen."

She stopped talking abruptly. She turned and smiled gently at her friend who had listened with such concern, "Hans, excuse me for burdening you. As I told you one of the first times we studied the Bible together, seeing the will of God is one thing, doing it, another."

31
Not "Why?" but "How?"

To this day Jane cannot explain how she knew that was her last performance in Naples, but suddenly she had a certain feeling "this is the end." When at the close of the last act, the audience stood, applauded, shouted and carried on as Italians do when they know they've heard great singing, Jane accepted her part of the ovation graciously, but as one in a trance.

She told no one that this was her last time on stage, because, in a sense, she scarcely believed it herself, but the "certain feeling" was there.

After a brief and stormy visit in Milan, she went to spend a few days in Switzerland. She intended to stay only a short while, but it turned out to be several weeks, as the Schaeffers were desperately in need of help because of illness. She did everything from washing dishes to digging in the garden and climbing a mountain to hanging out sheets while talking with young people and trying to answer their questions, "How do you know the Bible is true?" "What do you mean by sin?" "If there is a loving God, why are there so many tears in the world?" "Do you believe in a real Devil?" "Where does personality come from in the universe?" "What, you believe Adam and Eve were real people?"

The summer went quickly, and the opera singer returned to Vienna long enough to pick up some clothes and see if Hans was going on with the translation. She found him reading the Bible with enthusiasm which was something for the reserved Austrian.

She flew back to America in the autumn, and on the way to Virginia Jane stopped in New York to visit one of her sisters and her family. She arrived at night, and in the morning the children came tumbling into the guest room when they heard Aunt Jane was there. She was a favorite and they loved her visits because she was fun and always had something exciting to tell them about the interesting people she met, the things that went on in the opera world and the adventures she had travelling.

This time she opened up her Bible and gave them a vivid description of the tabernacle in the Old Testament. It had already become a special study for the singer, possibly because of the pageantry and splendor, the rich color and the wondrous aspect of it that speaks of the Messiah. After she closed the book, and the children had listened with close attention. one of her nieces said, "You know, Jane, after you've had your opera career you could become a missionary."

The child's innocent remark went deep into the heart of the singer. This is another reason, she thought, why I must give up opera now. How shameful of me to wait and give the Lord the leftovers of my life. The "Why" continued to get brighter, but the "How" to renounce her career became dimmer and dimmer.

For Jane the next few months were torture. There were further auditions and appearances on TV, where, on the outside she appeared to be the successful, radiant opera star, but in her soul there was warring and dreadful discord. She was not capable of making the decision, and the longer she delayed, the more impossible it got. Her Lord seemed far away.

On several occasions when she was home she attempted to tell her parents that she could no longer go on in opera, but then her father, normally a quiet and very modest man, would make a comment that showed how proud he was of her success. And she had never seen her mother happier—she couldn't find the words. What was additionally exasperating, she had nothing concrete to tell them. It sounds most unconvincing in the twentieth century to say you are giving up a successful career "to follow God."

One of her last nights at home, she cried out in agony, "O God, I haven't the courage nor the wisdom nor the faith to make this decision. If I am to give up my career, show me HOW...."

Finally the time came for Jane to return to Vienna. Her mother and father took her to the train. They both knew she was having a terrible struggle about something. You don't hide these things from parents. Her father particularly seemed to grasp that Jane would soon be living a different life, and the last thing he said to her as she boarded the train, "Don't forget your music!" The words were spoken gently, with compassion, and Jane never forgot them. They were the last words her father spoke to her.

When Jane arrived in Paris, she decided to stop off in Switzerland before resuming her studies in Vienna. Soon she was aboard a smaller, twin-engine plane bound for Geneva. She recalled that the airplane seemed abnormally noisy on the takeoff. As the plane approached Switzerland, Jane was still struggling with her awful burden. She had her Bible open on her lap and was reading and praying through a portion of Psalm 119. She paused to look out of the window at the white mountain peaks sparkling below. How cold and sharp they appeared in the moonlight, she thought, and how near, and, as Jane herself explained it in a letter to her parents—after it was all over, "You will be

164

a bit surprised to know that for the moment I am in Switzerland and am expecting to stay here until February 10th in order to make some very important decisions as well as to help out while the Schaeffers are away. The decision, of course, is whether I as a Christian should go on singing in the opera world ... knowing all the compromises one must make in one's own moral standards in order to do so.

"From the moment of my conversion on April 2nd, 1956 I have gradually come more and more to see that one has only one life to live and only that which is done to the glory of the Lord has any real eternal value. Shortly after taking off from Paris for Geneva in a twin-engine Swissair plane one of the engines broke down and for the next hour I was as close to death as I've ever been. My prayer during this terrifying time was that if God allowed us to land safely, I would give the rest of my life into His hands and follow His will for my life. In "The Lord's Prayer" we repeat over and over "Thy will be done," but do we really mean it???

"I feel sure it was a miracle that we landed safely, and when we finally came down there was emergency crash equipment all over the field. I shall always remember with horror the dreadful silence of that dead engine and the feeling of regret in my heart for the little I had done to show my gratitude to the Lord that He had taken my sins upon Himself and given me the gift of everlasting life.

"This is a time of difficulty and decision for me and I just hope you will be able to understand. It is something I have thought about for a long time with deep concern also for your feelings and for all you have done in the past to be such a great help to me...."

The letter was sent Special Delivery Air Mail, and as Jane said, "It was the most prayed-over letter I have ever written, and the one to Maestro—oh, the tears I shed."

Jane did go to Huemoz after the near plane crash.

The Schaeffers had no idea and she had no idea that L'Abri would become her life work. This the Lord worked out gradually, step by step, but they did need her help right away.

She spent her first days as a worker at L'Abri writing letters to sever all connection with opera. She would write a few words, then pace about the tiny room, at times crying loudly, praying earnestly, biting her fingernails. When the first tear-stained letter to her parents was finished, she began to write to Maestro. She got as far as "My dear Maestro ..." and broke down. It took three days to finish the letters, and it took six months before Maestro could even hear the name "Bella Salamona" without tears coming to his eyes.

Once the letters were written and mailed the Lord gave to the former opera singer a quietness of heart and mind, and assurance that she could leave the future of these loved ones in His hands, as much as she trusted Him for her future. With that Jane left her weeping behind and plunged into the work at hand, and it is never difficult to find work to do at L'Abri.

A sophisticated, blonde guest who had heard that Jane formerly sang in opera looked with pity at her one day on her knees vigorously scrubbing the steps of Chalet Melezes.

"What are you going to do now that you've given up opera?" demanded the blonde as she daintily but swiftly stepped back to avoid getting splashed.

"I'm doing it!" was the answer from the new missionary.

32
A Fulfilling Life

If you should visit Huemoz in the spring or summer, you might make the same mistake as the Smith College girl interested in music and who wanted to meet the former opera singer. She noticed someone working in the cornfield in front of Chalet Chesalet and she called down and asked in French where she could find Miss Smith. Jane pushed back her bright green straw hat and said with a warm smile, "I'm right here." Ever since she has been known as the "ardent gardener."

One must not get the false impression that all the singer does at L'Abri is scrub floors and hoe corn. She does do more than her share of these tasks because they are there and need to be done, and she has been disciplined to hard work since childhood, but the Lord who created Heaven and earth never wastes the talents He has given to His creatures.

With her various abilities, plus her singing, her genuine enthusiasm, her capacity to get things done and her faith in the Living God, Jane is now a vital part of L'Abri Fellowship. She uses practically every part of her training in opera in her present varied and exciting work, even Maestro's advice to "use big gestures, be definite with all movements and sing as if it is the most important thing in the world."

To give a glimpse of the international scope of L'Abri and the importance of knowing several languages, Jane was teaching a Bible class in Zurich one weekend when someone made the discovery that the twelve people gathered around the table for the study were from ten different countries.

When Chalet Chesalet was added to L'Abri, Jane moved across the road from the Schaeffers to be the hostess there. At that time, Chesalet was charming in the summertime, but with no central heating, only an ugly, black stove in the kitchen, it was a cold, damp dungeon the other three seasons. The former warrior, Brunnhilde, and the nineteenth-century stove had frightful battles. The singer usually lost. One dismal, cold morning when the noble Brunnhilde was trying to liven up the now dead fire she had carefully laid the night before by beating the stove with a broom handle, the pipe leading to the outside crashed to the floor. Several years later when central heating was finally installed in the chalet it was one of her finest hours, an occasion for great praise and thanksgiving to God for His goodness.

Besides being in charge of Chesalet which includes preparing and serving many meals, Jane teaches the Bible. Anyone who enjoys studying the Scriptures as much as she does makes a stimulating teacher. There will be many people, including myself, who will be everlastingly thankful to the former opera singer because she has helped us discover the joy and power that comes through concentrated, persistent study and appreciation of God's Word.

Even after she moved to Huemoz and had access to the L'Abri library, Jane continued to write to London for more books. As students started to come to Huemoz in greater numbers, they too needed more books, and today there is a branch of The Evangelical Library in Huemoz and Jane is in charge.

Also in the list of "what does she do now that she is no longer singing in opera," it should be noted that she spends many hours each week talking to guests. In a world bent on forgetting the individual man, those at L'Abri feel it is important to listen and to talk with the visitors personally. This Jane does willingly, as exhausting as it is sometimes. She vividly remembers what it meant to her that Maria Theresa, Georgia and the L'Abri family took time with her and considered her questions important.

Then, in spite of the fact that she had never pushed a wheelbarrow before she came to Switzerland, Jane now gardens and hovers over the chickens in the Chesalet woodshed with the same enthusiasm as she presents a lecture on Bach, Stravinsky, modern art or electronic music, or sings a solo in church or goes on a concert tour with the L'Abri Ensemble in Portugal, England, Sweden or America.

She continues to believe strongly in prayer and as she was reading her Bible and praying one day, she was reminded of her costumes packed in several trunks stored in Signora Rolandi's attic. These costumes were not only elaborately and beautifully made, really museum pieces, but they represented something personal and precious to Jane. Suddenly, as she stood that morning looking at the property below Chesalet which had been purchased for a chapel, she prayed that her costumes might be sold to help build the little church so badly needed now that the community was growing. As she explained it to her parents in a letter, "As for my costumes, they have been in my mind and of course I have loved them and have felt about them as some people do about their children, but God deals with us in mysterious ways and sometimes requires things of us that humanly speaking are difficult to give up. I so often think of the marvelous twenty-second chapter in Genesis where God asks Abraham to sacrifice his beloved son, knowing he was the thing Abraham loved most. Abraham didn't stand back for six months or a year questioning and doubting God, but "rose up early in the morning" to obey. Because of this glorious obedience Abraham is the spiritual Father of the invisible church of Christ....

"Be that as it may, I am considering selling my costumes. It will be painful to do, but there is no reason to keep them as dust collectors!!"

Very humanly she added, "However, I shall always keep my lovely diamond ring and please continue insurance on my fur coat as well."

Jane and Edith Schaeffer prayed together about the possibility of finding the right buyer for the costumes. It seemed, even to them, an impossible request, but one day a telegram came informing Jane that a singer wanted to look at her costumes. She was interested in only one or two, and so with little expectation Jane went to Milan to meet the singer.

First she tried on one, then another, and another, and to their amazement, all fitted perfectly and were far more beautiful than she had thought they would be. She bought everything, everything except the ostrich plumes which Jane sent to her mother.

33
Still Singing

Often the question is asked, "But does Jane still sing?" Those at Bellevue have one answer. They live in a large, pleasant chalet located directly above Chesalet and next door to Chalet les Melezes. It is a home for children who have cerebral palsy. One Sunday Jane carried up her autoharp and told the children that she was going to teach them some of her favorite hymns. That was the beginning of the Sunday Music Hour. As you watch faces, it is difficult to decide who enjoys the singing the most, those listening or the one singing.

Another person very aware that Jane still sings is Herr Lengacher, The Beeman. He moved to the mountains many years ago because of illness and lives in the chalet nearest to Chesalet. The tall, stooped stranger made no attempt to get acquainted in the Swiss-French village, preferring the companionship of his sheep and bees. He spent long hours planting an orchard, renovating his old chalet and making plans to build a new one.

One day as the solitary one, who has a knowledge and appreciation of nature, was grafting branches into his apple tree, he heard music coming from the dark-brown chalet across the field from him. He had never heard such beautiful music.

It took great effort and discipline for Jane to begin practicing again in the midst of the hubbub of life at L'Abri, but she knew if she did not vocalize regularly she would lose her voice. She lost heart, now and then, when month after month went by and she had no other outlet for her singing other than unto the Lord Himself amid the pots and pans in the Chesalet kitchen and to the children at Bellevue on Sundays. The church services for those at L'Abri were still being held in the Melezes' living room which was too small a space for Jane's Wagnerian voice, but the singer had faith that in the Lord's timing, He would provide a place for her to sing, even in Huemoz. And she intended to be ready, so practice she did, as regularly as possible in spite of many interruptions and difficulties.

What Jane did not know was that even in those practice hours she had an audience. One morning a friend of Jane's on the way to Chesalet saw the giant, stooped man leaning on his rack. Tears rolled down his cheeks as he listened to Jane singing, "O Divine Redeemer."

Finally, the Beeman, who rarely visited anyone in the village, asked a neighbor if she knew who sang so beautifully in the chalet next to his. They were standing in his orchard looking towards Chalet Chesalet when suddenly the kitchen door opened and Jane and Edith Schaeffer hurried up the path.

The village lady said, "The tall one is the singer," as Jane and Edith rushed up the road to Melezes. Then, as Herr Lengacher tells it, "The beautiful singing stopped and the tall one flew away, and I thought I'd never be able to thank her for her wonderful music." What he did not know, Jane had been called to Virginia for the funeral of her father.

After many months, the singing in Chesalet began again. Now it was winter, and in order to hear better, the Beeman pushed open his kitchen windows and sat in the chilly room and listened. Again tears moistened his weathered cheeks as the clear, high notes of "O Holy Night" rang across the field into his lonely, empty heart.

Spring came swiftly to the Swiss mountain village that year and everyone hurried outside. One lovely morning after he had heard "his concert," the Beeman walked slowly across the field and introduced himself to the singer, who was now outside planting onions. They spoke formally at first in French until Jane learned that her neighbor was Swiss-German. And they have been talking ever since in big, booming German.

Jane discovered that Herr Lengacher was an amazing person, wise, like her father, with knowledge and skill in several fields, and a man of wholesome, wonderful humor; and his admiration and appreciation for *his* neighbor led to his wanting to know in detail why she was hidden in the mountains when she should be singing for the world. This led to many conversations.

It did not come swiftly, nor was it easy, but in January, 1963, as the gentle giant and the former opera singer were reading together the first chapter of the Gospel of John, and she was speaking to him about the Creator Who sent His own Son as a Shepherd to find the lost, the Beeman, who had known much sadness in his life, entered the fold, never to be lost and lonely again. As Rosemary of Bellevue observed after his conversion, "I never knew Herr Lengacher was so tall!"

He does stand straighter and walks as a man who knows where he is going.

One evening, some time later, during the Sunday high tea in the Melezes' living room, the Beeman got out his wooden ruler, and in his slow, deliberate way stepped over students sitting and stretched out on the floor and the many other guests balancing tea cups in their laps and measured the long, narrow room.

"What you need is a chapel," the Beeman said. "And

173

my brother and I will build it." And they did.

Immediately the singer began talking about and praying for an organ. She did not vaguely pray for just any organ, she asked the Lord for a handmade, baroque organ to be designed by the great Dutch organ maker, Flentrop. Then being practical as well as mystical, she went out and bought some more chickens and began selling eggs in the community, "Fifty centimes a piece or two for a quarter!"

"But that is twice as much as they charge at the village store," complained an alto one night at choir practice.

"Of course," she said indignantly, "these hens are buying an organ."

Well, they didn't buy it all by themselves but they surely helped, and it encouraged other people to be generous givers too.

And so with a beautiful chapel, "high enough and long enough," according to the Beeman builder, "so that everyone can hear Jane sing her praise to God," and an exquisite, small organ built by Mr. Flentrop, music began to be an important part of L'Abri. It would take another book to tell of the many concerts—unusual concerts that have brought joy to so many people—to tell how music, which knows no language barrier, has spoken to village people and in many tongues and nations where words have failed; and how the L'Abri Ensemble came into being and has performed many times in the chapel and has made several wonderful tours in the United States and Europe. Through the music and the interest in all the arts at L'Abri many sensitive, talented people have been drawn to the tiny village in the Swiss Alps and the chapel has been and is used as a focal point for art festivals, music and art work shops with the emphasis on the truth that as we are made in the image of God, our Creator would have us be creative. Jane is the first person to say about these things and many more not recorded in this book, "Thanks be to God, the only wise God our Saviour, to Him be the glory."

Around the time Jane bought more chickens to help buy the organ, she wrote and asked Signora Rolandi to come to Huemoz for a visit. Signora, who had heard much about all that was going on at L'Abri, wrote and said that she would come only under the following conditions—that she be allowed to fix all the meals, do the dishes, mend, scrub, wash, iron and help with the chickens. Jane sent a telegram, "Come immediately and do as you please."

Signora came, did all that and more, and has been coming back every summer now for several years, not only because she enjoys the excitement at L'Abri and all the young people, but because she too, like the former opera singer, is singing a new song these days. As it says in Scripture, "And He hath put a new song in my mouth, even praise unto our God: many shall see it, and fear, and shall trust in the Lord" (Psalm 40:3).